walk into prehistory

Discovering over Forty of the Greatest
Ancient Sites of Britain and Ireland

Bill Bevan

FRANCES LINCOLN LIMITED
PUBLISHERS

This book is dedicated to my late parents: Irene Violet Bevan 1920–2010 and Arthur James Bevan 1915–64. My Mam instilled in me a will to achieve whatever I'd started and my Dad gave me an inspiration for photography from seeing his black and white prints while I was a child. I've needed both these qualities to complete this book.

HALF TITLE *Challacombe Stone Row, Devon*

TITLE PAGE *Dun Telve, Highland*

THIS PAGE *Ring of Brodgar, Orkney*

CONTENTS

N

Skara Brae ☆☆ ☆ Broch of Gurness
☆ Maes Howe

Dun Carloway ☆   ☆ Grey Cairns of Camster
Callanish ☆

Atlantic Ocean

Balnauran of Clava
☆ ☆ Loanhead
of Daviot

Glenelg Brochs ☆

North Sea

Kilmartin ☆
Achnabreck ☆

Yeavering Bell
☆

Beaghmore
☆   ☆ Long Meg and
Castlerigg ☆ ☆ her daughters
Navan ☆
Carrowkeel
☆ Rudston
Monolith
Loughcrew ☆ ☆ Newgrange
Hill ☆   ☆ Mam Tor
of Tara ☆ Bryn celli Ddu ☆ Arbour Low
☆   ☆
Tre'r ☆
Poulnabrone Ceiri ☆ ☆ Bryn Cader Faner

British
☆ Camp
Vragh Pentre   The
Ifan ☆   ☆ Ridgeway
☆ ☆ Foel Drygarn ☆
☆ Avebury
☆ Stonehenge

Grimspound
☆
Maiden Castle
Chysauster ☆
English Channel

PREFACE

Visiting all of the magnificent monuments in this book has taken me on many journeys across Britain and Ireland. I set myself the task of visiting all of them in one year, and dealing photographically with the weather that our variable Atlantic climate throws at us.

Sometimes I've started the day with a beautiful sunrise or waited – and waited – for the mist to lift and let the sunlight in; at other times I've waded through snow or been fortunate enough to catch a fleeting ray of sun among rain and storm clouds. With so many places spread across the whole of Britain and Ireland I have usually had only one or two visits to take the photographs. The only exceptions have been Stonehenge, which I visited over three years during the Stonehenge Riverside Project, and the sites found in my own backyard of the Peak District.

Many of the sites I knew already and revisited them as old friends. Some were places I had long wanted to see but had not yet got round to. One or two were places I hadn't heard of until I began researching this book or sites I came across on my travels.

The journey has been long and sometimes hard, such as when I had to lay up for a few days in Ireland to rest stiff and aching muscles, but it has always been more than rewarding. I have been to many magical places high on peaks to witness solitary sunrises above quiet lands. I have been there when frosts have still silvered the grass or mists have shrouded the hills. Likewise I've also been the last one at a number of places and seen the sun set, silhouetting the standing stones. I have travelled around Britain and Ireland in my campervan to get to the monuments in time for dawn.

There are, of course, many, many more ancient sites than those I've included in this book. I have had to make difficult decisions about which places to leave out, including some of my favourite prehistoric sites in Britain. I am sure there will be places you know well that you think should be in here. Where are, for example, the Rollright Stones or the Nine Ladies? Why none of the Cornish quoits or the Dartmoor reaves? Time and space constrictions, sadly, had to put a limit on the places I visited. I wanted to make sure I left enough space to write about the places to help the reader share the experience of being at them, rather than just produce another series of short, plain descriptions.

My aim for this book is for the words and photographs to work together to transport you to these amazing places, both today and when they were built. I want them to be brought alive as vibrant places occupied and inhabited in prehistory by people like you and me. I also want their modern settings, so often in some of our most beautiful countryside, to shine out.

I set two important criteria when choosing the places to visit – that photography could do them justice and that prehistoric people entered them along routes you can still see today, whether or not you can follow their exact routes. In most cases you can literally follow in the footsteps of ancient people but sometimes modern landholdings prevent this. There are also one or two sites in here where I have chosen to break my rules simply because I liked them so much.

So here you have some of my favourite prehistoric monuments, a fraction of the sites that survive from almost 4,000 years of prehistory. I hope you enjoy experiencing them through this book and that you may even be inspired to visit some of them.

Bill Bevan, Sheffield 2011.

INTRODUCTION

Walk Into Prehistory is a book about journeys: about some of the different types of journey prehistoric people made during their daily lives or ceremonies and about the journeys we can make today. Prehistoric communities travelled by walking as a matter of course, (not forgetting that this is the period when horses were first ridden), while today the only time we tend to walk any sort of long distances is for recreation.

Walk Into Prehistory brings together both forms of walking, and I hope you can use it to travel back in time, whether or not it inspires you to walk around the monuments I've chosen for the book. If you do visit any of the sites, the walks will enable you to better appreciate how they are set in their landscape and the ways they were approached in prehistory, compared to stopping at the nearest car park.

Each walk into prehistory is graded easy, moderate or difficult according to how strenuous it is, based on the length of the walk and the presence of steep slopes. There are, of course, car parks near by most of the monuments so if you can't walk the distances suggested in the routes you usually have a much closer option.

I have also indicated those sites that are accessible for people with low mobility or by childrens' buggies by parking in the nearby car parks, and places where the terrain may preclude buggies and mobility aids but are family friendly because the distances and ground makes them suitable for young children. Because

Walking along the line of an ancient route towards Mam Tor hillfort

Walk Into Prehistory is a large-format photographic book to enjoy at home, the routes and maps included are for guidance only, and you will need a good map for navigation; the relevant OS maps are listed for each walk.

One pleasure of visiting prehistoric monuments is that most of them are located in some of the most attractive corners of Britain and Ireland, the survival of both the monuments and the countryside being due to a lack of development over the last 200 years. Most, though not all, of the sites I've chosen for *Walk Into Prehistory* are found in the remoter uplands, some on the tops of hills. Their locations usually offer views across rugged hills, open moorland or rolling farmland, sometimes with backdrops of woodlands and occasionally lakes. Even if prehistory is not your passionate interest, a visit to any of these monuments is a way of exploring some of Britain and Ireland's most beautiful and varied landscapes.

The monuments vary immensely in scale and purpose, from the massive ceremonial arenas at Avebury, Newgrange, the Ring of Brodgar and Stonehenge, where thousands of people gathered from across a whole region to participate together in rituals, to settlements such as Chysauster, Dun Carloway and Grimspound, where families spent their daily lives.

The types of walk and experience you can have at each differ hugely too. You can still follow parts of known processional routes linking Avebury with the Sanctuary and Silbury Hill, Stonehenge with Durrington Walls or the Ring of Brodgar with the Stones of Stenness. The avenue used to approach Callanish thousands of years ago still stands, while the entrances at Arbor Low show the directions from which communities came to this henge with its fallen stone circle. By walking along these avenues and in through the entrances you are able to experience something of the large ceremonial sites as prehistoric people would have done, accepting that the changes in the landscape and our understanding of the world mean we can't fully get into the minds of our ancient ancestors. The most famous of these sites still attract huge gatherings, though today visitors come in their

hundreds of thousands or millions from all across the world.

At settlements like Chysauster, Grimspound and the great Iron Age brochs at Carloway, Orkney and Glenelg you can still walk in and out of doorways to enter rooms and houses which were once alive with families talking, laughing, shouting, cooking and working around hearths. At Chysauster you can wander along a street between houses, while at the

ABOVE *The outer ring of Stonehenge is about 4,500 years old*

OVERLEAF *Uragh stone circle is set in the beautiful Kerry countryside*

brochs you are still able to climb stairs which wind their ways up inside the stone walls of the towers. Settlements give a more personal connection to the past, where we can imagine what everyday life would have been like at home.

Hillforts give an all together different view of the past. The likes of Foel Drygarn, Maiden Castle, Mam Tor and Yeavering Bell were built during the Iron Age with strong rampart walls on the tops of high windswept hills where today's visitors wonder what on earth brought people to live in such exposed places. Often there is little to see except for the ramparts, the houses which sheltered inside mostly surviving solely as faint platforms which can be difficult to make out, though stone-built houses stand out well on Tre'r Ceiri. Even at hillforts, you can still walk in through original entrances and visualise open grassy hills as bustling villages packed full of houses and activity.

Much darker experiences can be sought by following the Neolithic equivalent of shamans and priests deep underground along narrow passages to the burial chambers at Bryn Celli Ddu, Camster, Carrowkeel, Loughcrew and Newgrange where the defleshed bones and cremated bodies of the deceased became the spirits of communal ancestors.

Remember to take a torch, and you will wonder at how prehistoric people crawled along the passages with only tallow candles or brushwood torches for light.

Walk Into Prehistory encompasses approximately 4,000 years of prehistory, a mind-bogglingly long period of our past, the end of which is quite a long time ago in itself. Prehistory officially ends with the first use of writing, which makes the 'end of prehistory' a moveable feast in Britain and Ireland. In what are now England and Wales, prehistory ends with the Roman invasion of AD 43, however in Ireland and Scotland, where the Romans didn't invade or hold their empire, prehistory is generally considered to end around AD 400 or later. I have largely taken the Roman invasion as my cut-off point for the date of the latest sites, with the Scottish brochs and Chysauster being the only monuments occupied after this time.

Archaeologists divide prehistory into three major periods based on the introduction and use of different materials for tools, with the Stone Age being followed by the Bronze Age and the the Iron Age.

Stone Age Britain begins with the arrival of the first humans about 250,000 years ago and is itself divided into three periods, though it is only during

the New Stone Age – or Neolithic – that permanent monuments in stone and earth began to be built.

The classification of prehistory into three ages originates in the 1820s, when the defining materials were some of the most obvious to survive, and while it is still used, today's archaeologists acknowledge that human culture didn't change dramatically with the introduction of new materials or even that it is solely these materials which define what society was like during each period. The prehistoric past was as complex and varied as more recent history, and certainly much more complicated than its division into Stone, Bronze and Iron intimates but a brief overview of the archaeological periods helps to give a timeline for the monuments in the book.

The Neolithic dates from between 4000 and 2500 BC, and is defined as the period when humans first domesticated animals and plants in order to own and control their food supply through farming rather than hunting and gathering. People made arrowheads, spear heads, scrapers, knives, awls, borers, axes, ards and a variety of other tools from flint and stone to use alongside wooden tools. They also made ceramic pots for mundane chores such as cooking and storing food, and for drinking alcohol and hallucinogens during ceremonies at henges and chambered tombs.

Families lived in small villages of timber rectangular houses, such as at Durrington Walls, or the more enduring stone buildings on Orkney. The first farmers cemented their relationship with the land and their rights to live and farm places by building chambered tombs inside large and often ornate stone mounds where they conducted rituals which altered the bones of the recently deceased into ancestors. These monuments to community, land rights and the ancestral past appear by 3000 BC and are the earliest permanent human-built structures found in most of Britain and Ireland, where people chose stone for many of their ceremonial monuments and timber for their houses.

They include Bryn Celli Ddu, Carrowkeel, Knowth, Loughcrew, Maes Howe, Newgrange, Pentre Ifan, Poulnabrone, West Kennet Long Barrow and Wayland's Smithy among many others. It is only on Orkney where easy-splitting flagstone is in such abundance and timber so scarce that we are able to visit Neolithic houses with standing walls at Skara Brae and, to a lesser extent, at Barnhouse near the Stones of Stenness.

One thing that nearly all of these tombs have in common is an alignment on the rising or setting sun or moon at the solstices. The entrances of most tombs face sunset or sunrise during either midwinter or midsummer, with the best-known solar event being the midwinter sunrise which lights up the end of the chamber deep inside Newgrange – when the weather permits of course. The farmers who built these tombs relied on the sun for life, and needed to worship its disappearance or reappearance to ensure its ongoing passage across their skies, especially during the darkest day of midwinter when the return of the sun to the northern hemisphere was probably the most critical event in the annual cycle of life and death.

Later in the Neolithic, communities began to build the first of the great henges and stone circles as places for large communal gatherings, which often but not always replaced the tombs as the focal points for ritual. Many smaller circles and henges sprang up all over Britain and Ireland to serve as ceremonial centres for families and local communities. The construction and use of henges and circles continued for over 1,500 years between 3000 and 1500 BC, covering not only the later Neolithic but also the early part of the Bronze Age, and so bridging the artificial division between periods that archaeologists had created by using tools as the basis of their prehistoric chronology.

The Bronze Age in Britain begins about 2500 BC with the first dated use of bronze tools, but also sees funerary rites changing as the communal placement of bones and cremations in chambered tombs for use in ancestor rites gives way to burial in individual graves under mounds, often along with bronze objects and a new type of pottery known as a beaker. This suggests that society became more hierarchical over this period. This seemingly dramatic change has encouraged a fierce debate in archaeology as to whether there were a 'Beaker' people who migrated from continental Europe or the adoption of a new package of objects by existing elites. A ground-breaking project at the University of Sheffield has begun to use radio-isotopes to identify where the people buried with beakers were brought up as children to try to answer this question.

Also during the Bronze Age, farming and settlement gradually became more sedentary and more fields were enclosed within boundaries, while flint and stone still continued to be used for most everyday

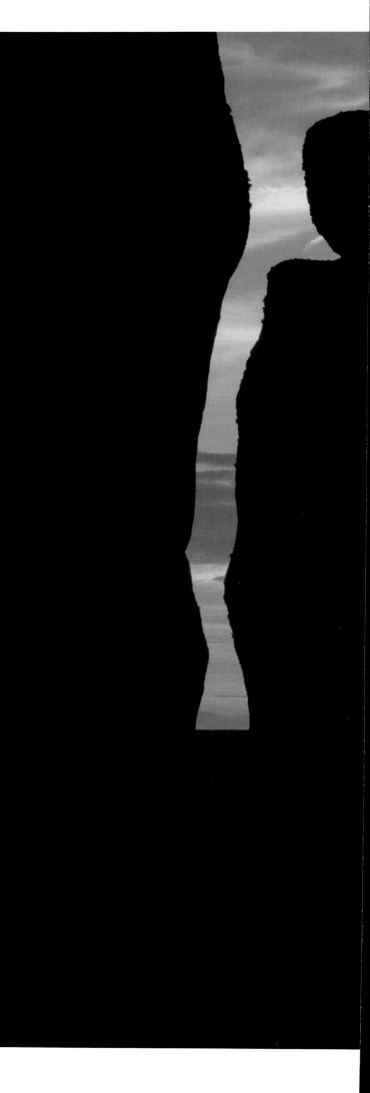

Arbor Low is one of the more distinctive henges of Britain

tools. Bronze was a precious metal, sometimes used for certain tools such as axes, but more often given as gifts, hoarded and ceremonially deposited in lakes, bogs or rivers. Leaders demonstrated their privileged position acquired through long-distance contacts and ability to exchange other materials for bronze by giving these precious objects to the gods.

Stonehenge takes it name only in part from the famous standing stones, the 'henge' suffix referring to the bank and ditch enclosing the stone circle, a pattern which can be seen again at Arbor Low, Avebury, Brodgar, Stenness and, before the circle was removed prior to the construction of the tomb, at Bryn Celli Ddu. Henges usually have two opposing entrances through a stone and earth bank surrounding a ditch, though some, such as Avebury, have four entrances while Stonehenge and Stenness have only one.

Stone circles probably represent most people's idea of a prehistoric monument, in no little part due to Stonehenge, but also because they are found across

much of Britain and Ireland. They vary enormously in size, as well as in the shape and height of their stones. Stones standing less than 2 metres (6½ ft) high are commonplace but the giant stones of prehistoric circles – Avebury, Brodgar, Callanish, Stenness and Stonehenge – are more impressive by their scarcity. Sometimes, as at the recumbent stone circles of Aberdeenshire, the largest stones were deliberately laid horizontally to create false horizons to observe the moon.

Arbor Low, Castlerigg and Long Meg and Her Daughters probably all served communities collecting together from smaller regions – the southern Peak District, northern Lake District or Eden Valley. Smaller still are places such as Beaghmore and Uragh, along with countless other circles, which were built and used by one or more families from the local area.

Similar astral alignments have been promoted and discussed for henges and stone circles as have been observed for tombs, with Stonehenge clearly being built to enable viewers to watch the midwinter solstice if not the midsummer one too. It is more difficult to identify such a strong position for most stone circles as no others have the same precise architecture of Stonehenge. However, even here there are clues such as the south-west facing recumbent stones seen so well at Loanhead of Daviot or the presence of the taller Long Meg outside the south-west facing entrance of her ring of daughters.

Another shared characteristic of tombs, henges and circles of all sizes is that they brought people from a community or communities together in shared labour to build them in the first place. Joint construction projects, whether grand or small, created a strong sense of community identity and of belonging among the people who worked alongside each other to dig out ditches, pile stones and earth into banks, haul stones across the landscape and erect the stones in the right locations.

Whether these projects were undertaken under communal agreement or the leadership of people with social and religious power, the effect was the same – to bind individuals, families and wider communities together through both physical exertion and universally held beliefs. These ties were reinforced every time people gathered for ceremonies and helped to maintain the monuments by clearing out the ditches. Henges and stone circles of all sizes, from Avebury to Uragh, were as much about celebrating the wider community as they were about honouring ancestors or gods.

The Bronze Age wasn't all ceremonies and moon-gazing however, and there are many enclosed settlements or villages comprising a number of round houses within a walled or fenced boundary. Most of these are only known through excavation, their timber buildings and palisades long-since rotted and ploughed over.

In some upland areas we find stone traces where field boundaries and house foundations were made from stone, partly just to clear away stone from the ground to be able to cultivate it, and we are fortunate that some communities on Dartmoor chose to build substantial enclosed settlements with stone such as at Grimspound. There are also places such as Kilmartin and Clava where tombs were built during the Bronze Age which look, at least superficially, very much like

some of the Neolithic chambers and passages, further blurring some of the distinctions between the two periods.

By about 800 BC a new metal began to appear in Britain and Ireland, one that would eventually revolutionise crafts and farming by leading, for example, to iron-tipped ploughs capable of turning over heavier clay soils not previously worked. The boundary with the Bronze Age is, once again, not so clear-cut, with numerous settlements and hillforts originating in the late Bronze Age and continuing to be occupied during the early Iron Age.

One of the most identifiable monuments from the Iron Age is the hillfort, an enclosed upland site which usually crowns a ridge, hilltop or slope with impressive stone and earth ramparts that can be seen

TOP *Clava Cairns are Bronze Age tombs, often sited within a stone circle*

ABOVE *British Camp is a dramatic Iron Age hillfort, its ramparts etched into one of the Malvern Hills*

for miles. The more elaborate ramparts comprise massive parallel banks and ditches etched into the earth of the chalk downs in south-west England or in hills from the Malverns to the Peak District. Further west and north, ramparts tend to be large walls without accompanying ditches.

Hillforts sometimes contained a village while others seem to have been used for ceremonies or corralling livestock. Some hillforts began life in the Bronze Age, such as Mam Tor, while others originated later in the Iron Age, including British Camp, Foel Drygarn, Maiden Castle, Tre'r Ceiri, Uffington Castle and Yeavering Bell. Even the hillforts purely Iron Age in date usually enclose a hilltop used during the early Bronze Age for burial mounds, suggesting a continuation or revisiting of specially venerated hills. Harking back to what would even then have been an ancient funerary monument may have been an important part of claiming some form of ancestral right to settle on the hill and build impressive ramparts.

The term hillfort was coined by Victorian archaeologists who saw these great Iron Age ramparts as analogous to medieval castles and imperial forts designed to withstand sieges by standing armies. We now know that Iron Age warfare wasn't organised along quite such militaristic lines, but was a combination of bravado, display, shock tactics, one-to-one battles, skirmishes and general melees. Hillforts weren't built so much to defend their occupants against sustained sieges as to prevent any enemies even considering attacking the community in the first place, or to provide a safe haven when fighting did break out.

Hillforts were as much about display and symbolism as they were about defence. The bringing together of large numbers of people to build and maintain the ramparts symbolised the strength of the community, and possibly some form of allegiance to a leader or single family, while the scale of the ramparts showed to others how strong and important the whole community was – a way of testifying its right to occupy part of the landscape.

Iron Age settlements you can visit are rare. Most houses were built in timber and have long rotted away, leaving only floors and post holes preserved underground. There are some exceptions, with the stone towers of Scotland's brochs the most evocative and impressive prehistoric buildings to survive

in Britain. People preferred stone over timber in other regions too, such as Cornwall's West Penwith peninsula, leaving us villages at places like Chysauster where you can wander in and out of houses with walls standing to head height or more.

The Iron Age in England and Wales officially ends with the coming of the Roman occupation in AD 43, which brought new cultural ideas and the first documentary records of Britain. The Irish and Scottish Iron Ages are considered to last until the coming of Christianity and use of writing from approximately AD 400 onwards. Southern Britain's Roman interlude may be seen more as an aberration when put in the context of the rest of Britain and Ireland and, in many ways, is as much as continuation of the Iron Age under Roman occupation as it is a new period called Roman Britain.

The organisation and cultures of the Roman Empire certainly had their impact, though, whether on the level of the development of towns and roads, the interaction between local communities and novel social ways or the adoption of religious practices. Roman Britain was an amalgam of regional traditions and Roman imports, this mix often inspiring the creation of new cultural ways of living such as bringing new gods into local pantheons.

For the purposes of this book, the Roman invasion is a convenient date to finish our journey around prehistoric Britain and Ireland, though the lack of finality between what we might call the 'end of prehistory' is reflected in the inclusion of places such as Chysauster and the Scottish brochs, which originated in the Iron Age but continued into the first decades or centuries AD.

We begin our journey into prehistory along one of England's best-known long-distance routes. The Ridgeway is 87 miles of footpath and bridleway along the chalk uplands of the Chilterns and North Wiltshire Downs beginning on the Hertfordshire and Buckinghamshire border in the east before running through Berkshire and Oxfordshire to end in Wiltshire in the west. This icon of the modern recreational route devoted to walking for pleasure and exercise originates, though only in part, thousands of years earlier and passes many of the types of prehistoric monuments we'll encounter elsewhere in Britain and Ireland. It is a fitting introduction to the prehistory of these isles.

OPPOSITE *Dun Carloway on the Isle of Lewis is one of Scotland's stunning Iron Age brochs*

SOUTHERN ENGLAND

WALKING THE PAST
THE RIDGEWAY

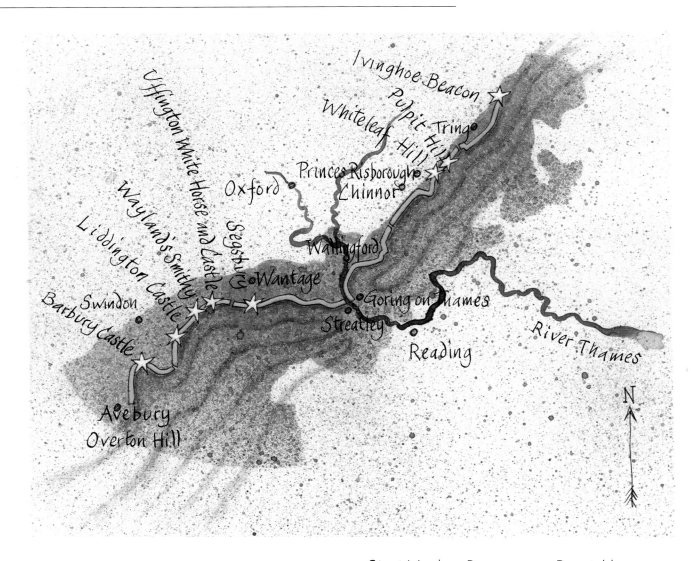

The Ridgeway follows the chalk ridges of the Chilterns and North Wiltshire Downs, which are bisected by the River Thames at Goring Gap. Today the whole length of these uplands is threaded by the Ridgeway long-distance National Trail. Since they were on open ground above the thickly wooded valleys and plains, like the other great bands of chalk which cross southern England, they were natural choices as pathways in prehistory too. Whether the Ridgeway was thought of as a single route or a multitude of separate routes in prehistory is unknown, but what is beyond doubt is the importance of the open chalk ridge to prehistoric peoples.

The easternmost point of the Ridgeway begins on

Start Ivinghoe Beacon, near Dunstable

Site location SP960169 and SU120682, OS Explorer 1:25,000 maps 157, Marlborough and Savernake Forest; 170, Abingdon, Wantage & Vale of White Horse; 171, Chiltern Hills West, and 181, Chiltern Hills North

Length 87 miles

Time 6 days

Difficulty Moderate

Plenty of opportunities for shorter half-day walks at key prehistoric monuments

The view over the Vale of Aylesbury from Ivinghoe Beacon, Hertfordshire, at the eastern end of the Ridgeway

Ivinghoe Beacon, a small promontory at the end of the undulating chalk ridge of the Chilterns, crowned with the ramparts of an Iron Age hillfort. This is one of the best places to discover what hillforts are about, even though the remains of the earthworks today look pretty insignificant. There are far more impressive hillforts further west on the Ridgeway, but what makes Ivinghoe Beacon special is the view.

The vast expanse of the Vale of Aylesbury stretches before you to the north and west as far as Aylesbury, Leighton Buzzard and Milton Keynes. What you see is a quintessentially southern English rural landscape of patchwork fields, grazing sheep, wheat fields and tidy villages of red brick cottages, pubs and manor houses, some of which have thatched roofs. This is a very modern landscape yet it is one that speaks to us of timeless tradition.

This is one of the few times we will encounter such a stereotype of the English countryside. From now on most of our journey takes us north and west to more rugged, upland landscapes where the absence of the plough in more recent times and the presence of good building stone throughout prehistory have combined to bequeath us some of the greatest testaments to the achievements of our ancient ancestors.

Much of the Ridgeway along the Chilterns runs through wooded slopes above fields and towns, while on the Wiltshire Downs the landscape opens up with

ABOVE *The Iron Age ramparts of Uffington Castle, Oxfordshire, controlled access along the Ridgeway where it ran along the Berkshire Downs*

RIGHT *The wood-cloaked slopes below the ramparts of the Iron Age hillfort on Pulpit Hill, Buckinghamshire*

views across grassland and arable fields. Along the route of the Ridgeway can be found Neolithic tombs, Bronze Age burial mounds, Iron Age hillforts and the famous Uffington White Horse.

Whoever controlled the hillforts controlled access along the ridge-top route during the Iron Age. Different communities would have lived in these well-defended sites; some are known settlements though others have no evidence for occupation. Warfare during the Iron Age consisted largely of small-scale skirmishes and was more about display, bravado and heroism than large armies conducting sieges. Hillforts made communities safe against such warfare and provided controlled passing points to check any unknown traveller. The local head families accrued material wealth and standing through 'taxing' passing traders. These material goods trickled down to other families in the community, and a head family's social standing was maintained for as long as it was able to

LEFT *Uffington White Horse, Oxfordshire, and the views north from the Ridgeway across the Vale of the White Horse*

bring in 'wealth' and redistribute it.

All of the Ridgeway's hillforts stood sentinel over large views, and just as importantly, could themselves be seen from many miles around. Travelling east to west we encounter Ivinghoe Beacon, Pulpit Hill, Segsbury, Uffington, Liddington and Barbury, all commanding high points, with Uffington on one of the the highest hills in Oxfordshire. The local communities recognised the stark aesthetic and symbolic potential of their land, keeping the ramparts clean to ensure that the white chalk made their hillforts prominent for miles around.

Uffington's famous white horse dates from around 1400–800 BC, some 500 years older than the hillfort. Its creators carved out trenches in the chalk hillside then packed them with more chalk to create an intriguing monument. While the beautifully stylised horse can be seen from the vale below, it is really directed skywards, pointing to the heavens. Below is the flattened chalk mound known as Dragon Hill.

Legend has it that it was here that St George slew the dragon and the dragon's blood poisoned the ground – which is why there is an unusual bare patch on its surface. Dragon Hill was probably an arena for ceremonies related to the horse. The acoustics are perfect; sound carries clearly between the Manger, the dry coomb below the horse, Dragon Hill and the Horse, so people could have gathered in the Manger to hear ceremonies conducted on Dragon Hill.

Treading further back in time, thousands of years before the Iron Age, a Neolithic community buried the bones of their ancestors in a small wooden chamber under a mound which was later extended to create the long mound with the south-east-facing stone chamber tomb known as Wayland's Smithy. Anglo-Saxon myths link the mound with Wayland the Smith who had an anvil here, and that if you left a horse by the tomb overnight with payment, you would find it shod in the morning.

The western end of the Ridgeway gradually drops down into the Kennet Valley to bring us to the giant Neolithic ceremonial complex focused on Avebury. Here the great monuments of Avebury, Silbury Hill and West Kennet, among others, formed stopping points for conducting rituals along a processional route beside the source of the River Kennet.

OPPOSITE *Wayland's Smithy, Oxfordshire, is a Neolithic chambered tomb on the route of the Ridgeway*

ABOVE *Avebury in Wiltshire marks one end of the Ridgeway, at the point where the Wiltshire Downs meet the Kennet Valley*

RING OF AGES
AVEBURY, WILTSHIRE

A visit to Avebury henge is a journey into one of the largest ceremonial monuments in Europe. The henge is so large that Avebury village fits inside its 420 metre (1,375 ft) diameter bank and ditch. The bank originally stood 9 metres (30 ft) high and the ditch had an equal depth.

Inside the henge are three sarsen stone circles. The largest circle comprised ninety-eight standing stones running around the inner circumference above the ditch and contained the two smaller circles, each 100 metres (328 ft) in diameter, inside it. Avebury was built over a 600-year period beginning with the bank and ditch around 3000 BC and finishing with two avenues in 2400 BC.

The henge is part of a vast late Neolithic to early Bronze Age ceremonial centre which straddles

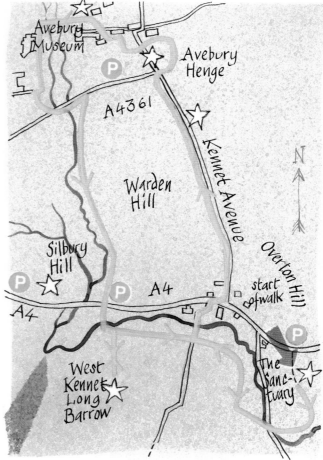

Start Overton Hill
Site location SU118680, OS 1:25,000
Explorer map 157, Marlborough &
Savernake Forest
Distance 5 miles
Time 3 hours
Difficulty Easy
Accessible

Some stones serve pubs rather than the other way round

almost 2½ miles of the River Kennet. Kennet Avenue, a routeway marked by two parallel lines of standing stones, links the south-eastern henge entrance with the Sanctuary over two miles to the south-east. To the south is West Kennet Long Barrow, one of the largest prehistoric tombs in Britain, and Silbury Hill, the largest human-made mound in Europe. These monuments were built and used for over 1,000 years, beginning 5,600 years ago in the Neolithic period. This vast landscape of ceremonial sites is best appreciated by walking between the main monuments, recreating where possible the routes of prehistoric processions.

I recommend beginning at the Sanctuary, once a monument of concentric timber circles which was built on Overton Hill 5,000 years ago and may have been a starting point for ceremonies culminating at Avebury. The hill overlooks the arable farmland of the wide, gently sloping Kennet Valley with views across the denuded rolling fields to West Kennet Long Barrow and Silbury Hill. Concrete blocks mark the positions of the long-decayed timbers.

Due to the modern roads it is not safe to follow directly in the footsteps of the prehistoric people who worshipped at Avebury. Instead, take a detour by heading south along the public footpath towards the village of West Kennet. If you walk through the village and pick up the minor road that runs north towards Avebury you will be able to follow close to the line of the Avenue. The chalkland slowly rises all the way from the Kennet to Avebury. Today it is an almost treeless landscape of large pastures and arable fields divided with hedges or fences. Five thousand years ago this would have been a more wooded landscape with large open clearings for grazing livestock and growing crops.

After a while you will see a double line of sarsens springing from the field to your left. This is the prehistoric Avenue and you can walk along this ancient route when you reach the National Trust open access land about half way to Avebury. If you look around you will notice that you are in a dry valley defined by the slopes of Avebury Down and Waden Hill which rise to either side.

Prehistoric people built the Avenue to monumentalise this natural routeway, using the dry valley to focus attention on their approach towards the henge, while hiding it until the last moment. Just

The view of Avebury from the bank near to the entrance at the end of the Kennet Avenue

as at Stonehenge, the Avebury henge is deliberately hidden beyond the brow of a hill for much of the length of its Avenue, to create a sense of anticipation among those in the procession. As you crest the hill today, one of the first things that will catch your attention is the graceful tower of Avebury's medieval church rising above treetops. About 4,000 years ago, you would have seen the two burial mounds which mark the skyline beyond the henge, while the bank blocked the view into the henge.

The last stretch of the Avenue snakes over to the left before turning back to the right to run towards the eastern entrance of the henge. By taking this route, the Neolithic builders deliberately heightened the drama of the approach, which finished with a view through the entrance towards the eastern stone circle. This

ceremonial and architectural focal point is displayed to the worshippers in much the same way as the first scene of a play is revealed to a theatre audience when the curtain is drawn back.

Continue along the Avenue through the entrance and into the stone circle, passing the massive monoliths of the perimeter circle on your way. One of these is known as the Devil's Stone and young women would sit on it on May Day eve to make a wish.

A detour up on to the bank gives a good vantage point to take in the sheer size of Avebury henge and the strange juxtaposition between prehistoric standing stones and medieval village. Whether you choose to walk around the top of the bank or stroll from one standing stone to another you are sure to be impressed by the scale of the design and effort that went into creating the henge and stone circles. Most of the stones were still standing in the 1600s, despite efforts by the Church to desanctify this pagan centre, but were subsequently broken up by people from Avebury village for building stone.

If you leave the henge along the western road through the village you exit via another original entrance which had an avenue almost exactly the same as Kennet Avenue leading to it. This avenue was taken down centuries ago and today only one stone survives. A footpath takes you down to another road then alongside the River Kennet, a shallow and narrow ditch here near its source. Its route was part of the Neolithic ceremonial way from Avebury to Silbury Hill, the flat top of which forms a striking destination on the footpath which follows this ancient route.

ABOVE *Silbury Hill is tall enough for its top to be visible above parts of the surrounding landscape*

OPPOSITE *The façade of West Kennet Long Barrow lit by the rising full moon*

At 37 metres (120 ft) high, Silbury Hill is the tallest prehistoric mound in Europe and comparable to some of Egypt's smaller pyramids. Begun in 2400 BC, once the henge and avenues were complete, it appears to be nothing more than a mound of chalk and clay. No burials have been found in the many tunnels dug inside by archaeologists keen to find a Pharaoh-like wealthy burial.

Instead, Silbury Hill is a massive statement to the identity and beliefs of the Neolithic community who deliberately built it high enough for its distinctive flat top to be visible above the rolling landscape to people living and working in and around the Kennet Valley. They seem to have built it as part of the ongoing creation of the ceremonial landscape, once they had finished their building work at Avebury.

You pass to the east of Silbury Hill, which looks striking in early morning light, to cross the A4 carefully and take the gentle incline up to West Kennet Long Barrow. The long, low mound silhouetted on the near skyline above the fields was built in 3600 BC and is the earliest monument of the Avebury complex.

As you approach closer you will see some of the sarsen stones that look like the broken teeth of a reclining behemoth. They form a façade to either side of the entrance to the stone-lined tomb. Dark chambers to either side once held the dismembered bones of over forty-six men, women and children. The façade faces the rising sun and would have been a backdrop to ceremonies held here to honour and inter ancestors for over 1,000 years, until the entrance was sealed some time after 2400 BC.

A legend tells of a ghostly priest with a huge white hound who visit the tomb on Midsummer's Day. From West Kennet Long Barrow you can take a footpath along the south side of the river back to the Sanctuary to complete your walk along this prehistoric ceremonial circuit.

PREHISTORIC ICON
STONEHENGE, WILTSHIRE

Start Woodhenge car park

Site location SO759400, OS 1:25,000 Explorer map 130, Salisbury and Stonehenge

Length 5½ miles

Time 3 hours

Difficulty Easy Accessible

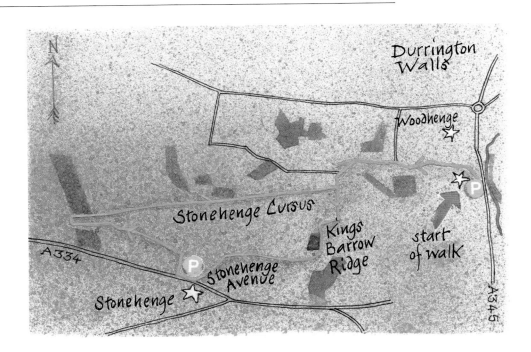

There is no more famous prehistoric monument in Britain than Stonehenge. The trilothons have become an icon of the ancient and mystical, attracting hundreds of thousands of people from all over the world each year to wonder how and why this elaborate circle of massive stones was built. Many of today's visitors are not aware of the prehistoric avenue that connected Stonehenge with the River Avon and, via the river, the even larger henge of Durrington Walls to the north-east.

There are two ways to appreciate the scale of Stonehenge. One is to book a visit inside the circle before or after normal opening hours, while the other is to walk towards it along the avenue.

By beginning at Durrington Walls, you can recreate a journey made by thousands of prehistoric people for hundreds of years. Even though the modern footpaths to Stonehenge do not follow the ancient processional route, you can still walk along the final part of the avenue to experience arriving at Stonehenge in much the same way as the prehistoric communities who gathered here thousands of years ago. The route also takes in the wider Stonehenge landscape which is packed full of the remains of other prehistoric monuments, ranging from a Neolithic cursus to burial mounds and long-decayed timber circles.

The 'walls' of Durrington Walls, the largest henge in Britain at over 500 metres (1,640 ft) in diameter, are the inner slope of the huge henge bank and the outer edge of the internal ditch - all that survive of a ceremonial monument whose scale is breathtaking.

The bank may originally have been over 5 metres (16½ ft) high and up to 30 metres (98 ft) wide, with the ditch sunk 5.5 metres (18 ft) into the chalk. There were two entrances, in the north-western and south-eastern sides, the latter connected to the River Avon only 60 metres (197 ft) away along a stone-laid avenue defined by a pair of banks and ditches.

The whole henge is built on sloping ground overlooking the river and would have been a magnificent sight for anyone approaching it this way, especially as the interior contained three timber circles with another timber circle located just outside at Woodhenge. While you can walk around inside Durrington, you cannot easily experience the south-eastern entrance because of the nearby A345, or follow the avenue, which is below the turf of a private field.

What is intriguing to imagine is a large village of Neolithic timber and thatched rectangular houses clustered outside the south-eastern entrance of the henge. Recent excavations by the University of Sheffield identified the village and the avenue, dating occupation to approximately 2600 BC – contemporary with the earliest stone circle at Stonehenge. It poses the intriguing question: was this where the builders of Stonehenge lived?

To walk to Stonehenge today we need to follow the single-track lane west, passing beside the concrete posts which mark the timbers of Woodhenge, a henge with a timber circle dating from about the same time as the stones were first raised at Stonehenge. More prehistoric timber structures and a standing stone once filled the blank pasture field on your left. A footpath on your left takes you across the higher ground above the Avon Valley.

TOP *Stonehenge is Britain's most iconic prehistoric monument*

ABOVE *The smooth-worn floor and charcoal-stained hearth of one of the Neolithic houses beside Durrington Walls*

One of the fortunate few was buried in this Bronze Age mound on King Barrows ridge overlooking Stonehenge from the east

As you near the trees you are approaching the end of the Stonehenge Cursus, a 3 km (1¾ mile) long monument, which has recently been dated by the Stonehenge Riverside Project to about 3500 BC from an antler pick used to dig the monument. This predates the earliest evidence at Stonehenge by 500 years and may be one of the earliest monuments in the Stonehenge area. This eastern terminal was marked by a long barrow this side of the trees, which has long since been ploughed over, though its 2 metre (6½ ft)

deep ditches survive below ground. The purpose of the Cursus is still unclear, though it appears to have been a route which was enclosed to prevent access to it perhaps because it was sanctified or even cursed.

Walking south along King Barrows Ridge takes you past a number of large Bronze Age burial mounds built between 2600 and 1600 BC, when Stonehenge was almost complete. When you reach the gap between two woods you are on the line of the avenue, which has climbed up the valley side from the River Avon to the

*Excavating the avenue's western ditch
as it approaches Stonehenge*

south-east, beginning at a small bluestone riverside henge before curving uphill in a great arc to reach the ridge. This is where the prehistoric communities gathering for ceremonies at Stonehenge would have caught their first sight of the stone circle, until now hidden.

Today you see a landscape of neatly short-cropped grass with conifer plantations sheltering army barracks to your right, the A303 cutting a noisy swathe to your left, and Stonehenge stuck between this and another road. More burial mounds dot the landscape all around Stonehenge, while the line of the much older Cursus stretches out straight beside the conifers to end in the gap in the plantation ahead. The landscape may be similar to when Stonehenge was at its height, minus the roads and conifer plantations, as Salisbury Plain was mostly open grasslands broken up with small deciduous woodlands, though perhaps not as neatly managed as today. It would certainly have been quieter without the constant rumble of traffic on the A303.

Sunset over Stonehenge from the avenue.
The tallest stone formed one half of a
frame for observing the sun and moon,
which stood above the outer ring of stones

You can now follow in the footsteps of the prehistoric builders and worshippers by walking along the route of the avenue as it crosses the large pasture. It runs in a straight line down into the dry valley, after which it turns towards the monument and once more climbs uphill. Faint ditches mark either side of the avenue from this point onwards.

One thing to notice is how Stonehenge disappears then reappears as you walk uphill until you are almost upon it, and it is revealed in all its splendour. Today you must take a detour via a gate near the visitor centre to cross the road and approach only as far as the fence allows. As this book went to press, ongoing plans to close the road and reunite Stonehenge with its landscape were still undecided.

The avenue meets Stonehenge's henge just beyond the fence beside a standing stone known as the Heel Stone. Legend tells that the Devil threw the stone at a friar who was running away from him and it struck the friar on the heel, hence the name. It is actually the survivor of a pair of stones that marked the end of the avenue, and so the arrival of prehistoric people at the stone circle. The avenue crossed the henge over a causeway, beyond which you can make out another stone lying flat. This was also one of a pair that framed the final entrance to the circle.

Stonehenge now stands before you, its outer ring of trilothons topped by lintel stones forming an impressive screen in front of the horseshoe of taller trilothons and the inner circle of bluestones. The monument you see today is the result of almost 1,500 years of construction and alteration between approximately 3000 and 1600 BC, as well as a subsequent 3,400 years of abandonment, neglect, collapse, stone-robbing, antiquarian rediscovery, reconstruction and management as a World Heritage Site.

The first structure to be built was the henge, enclosed within a ring of stones or timbers. In about 2600 BC the first bluestones were erected, possibly forming a double ring, then during the next 200 years the outer ring and inner horseshoe of sarsen stones was added. The outer ring is connected by a row of lintels resting on mortise and tenon joints, raising the height of the outer ring to almost 5 metres (16½ ft) above the ground.

The horseshoe comprises five trilothons, each a pair of massive stones topped with a lintel rising gradually in height from 6 metres (20 ft) to 7.3 metres (24 ft). The tallest trilothon was at the apex of the horseshoe towards the south-west and so on the opposite side of the circle from the end of the avenue. The effect was to create a window above the outer ring for people standing at the avenue to watch the passage of the sun and moon on their descents during the summer and winter solstices. Religious leaders would have orchestrated ceremonies from inside the circle, their rituals screened by the outer ring to enhance the sense of mystery.

Stonehenge was one of the most architecturally elaborate of all the grand stone arenas built by early farming communities for the theatre of ritual and the upholding of social power based on maintaining the passage of the sun across the skies. Recent research by Mike Parker-Pearson and the Stonehenge Riverside Project has developed the theory that ceremonial processions between Durrington Walls and Stonehenge were conceived by prehistoric people as journeys between the place for the living and the place for the dead, with Stonehenge built in stone to commemorate the permanence of the ancestors.

From Stonehenge you can continue to the western end of the Cursus, via a string of Bronze Age burial mounds, to then walk the full length of the Cursus back towards Durrington Walls. This is a great way to experience changing views of Stonehenge in its landscape.

OPPOSITE *One of the Welsh bluestones standing in front of a sarsen trilothon inside Stonehenge*

CASTLE IN THE AIR
MAIDEN CASTLE, DORSET

Start Dorchester
Site location SY689903,
    OS 1:25,000 Explorer
    map OL15, Purbeck
    and South Dorset
Distance 2.5 miles
Time 2 hours
Difficulty Moderate

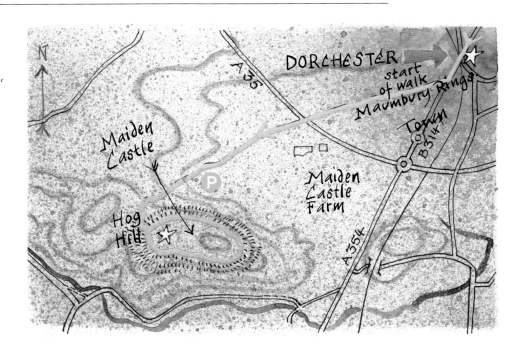

Maiden Castle is the largest and most complex Iron Age hillfort in Britain. Over 2,000 years ago it was home to a large, thriving population who lived in round houses densely packed within the mighty ramparts on top of the hill.

The hillfort was built in about 600 BC on the site of what had been a Neolithic causewayed enclosure over 2,000 years previously. Generations of people lived inside the hillfort's ramparts until the Roman conquest of Britain, when most of the population was moved to a new town called Durnovaria on the banks of the River Frome. This was to become modern Dorchester and today many of its inhabitants return daily to Maiden Castle to stroll, jog, walk their dogs or quietly take in the views on a quiet grassy hilltop which resounds to the song of skylarks and bleating of sheep.

You can easily walk to Maiden Castle from nearby Dorchester which is about 2.5 km (1½ miles) to the north-east. Follow Weymouth Road from the centre of town, passing Maumbury Rings on the way. This is a Neolithic henge adapted during the Roman period as an amphitheatre for the citizens of Durnovaria.

Turn right along Maiden Castle Road, where trees and suburban houses hide the hillfort until you are among the fields. Then you see the bulk of a low, flat-topped grassy hill above the chalkland, docked like an ocean liner among the fields. This is not a spectacular hill like those used for hillforts by the inhabitants of British Camp, Mam Tor or Tre'r Ceiri, but it is still the highest land above the river's flood plain. As you approach, heading to the car park just to the north of the hillfort if you prefer a shorter walk, you can make out the lines of the massive ramparts which circle the hill. Two thousand years ago the skyline would have been topped with a wooden palisade of tight-set timber posts on the highest rampart.

There are two paths on to the hillfort from the car park but only one follows in the steps of its Iron Age inhabitants which takes you through the dramatic western entrance. This entrance is a maze of paths winding through steep-sided ramparts and ditches, designed to confuse attackers as well as emphasise the importance of entering the hillfort. You switch back on yourself time and again and it is not immediately clear how you can navigate your way

Looking out across Maiden Castle's maze-like eastern entrance

through the maze. Only when you reach the top and look back can you truly get an idea of the entrance's complexity.

At the top of the entrance you can turn left to climb on top of the innermost rampart along the northern side of the hillfort. This makes a pleasant short circular walk that will give you views of Dorchester, Bincombe Down and, if it is clear, even the English Channel to the south. In the Iron Age all of these views would have been partly hidden behind the tall wooden palisade.

Look down and you really appreciate the scale of the earthworks which comprise three vertiginous ramparts separated by deep ditches on this side. These ditches and ramparts were built about 450 BC to replace a single rampart when the hillfort tripled in size to encompass the whole hill. These massive ramparts were built to demonstrate the status of the inhabitants as much as being defensive. Their scale goes far beyond what was needed for small-scale Iron Age warfare, so they could also be thought of as the nuclear deterrents of the day.

The grassy plateau inside the ramparts lies quiet today, home solely to a flock of sheep. Imagine

The complex of Maiden Castle's western ramparts

looking down on timber round houses packed close to each other over 2,000 years ago, their conical thatched roofs reaching a little above your head. People and animals would be continually moving along paths between the houses and the air was not caressed by the song of skylarks but resounded to the noisy hum of talk and work. Most of this work was agricultural. So much grain was stored in underground pits and on raised wooden granaries that the people of Maiden Castle, like many of the large hillforts of the south-west, must have been responsible for the centralised control of farming produce in this area.

If you continue along the uppermost rampart you will pass square stone walls which survive from a temple built towards the end of the Roman period in AD 367 or later. Eventually you reach the top of the eastern entrance, a place where the inhabitants of Maiden Castle may have witnessed one of the most dramatic events of the Roman invasion of Britain.

In AD 43, the wooden palisade would have been packed with people, their mood tense and excitable, as they waited for Vespasian's Roman army to arrive from over the low ridge to the east. The Roman army was fast approaching after defeating and accepting

OVERLEAF *The deep chalk-cut ditch between the top and central ramparts on Maiden Castle's northern side*

the surrender of Iron Age tribes between modern Dorset and Kent.

The people of Maiden Castle were not prepared or equipped for the new type of warfare they were about to encounter. Wearing no armour and most probably standing on top of the ramparts in acts of bravado, they would have made easy targets for the Roman ballista bolts. The Britons' main weapon of long-distance attack was the sling.

Archaeologists found thousands of sling shots hoarded in the round houses. But these would have been ineffective against a well-drilled armoured army. Vespasian won. We don't know for sure whether

Vespasian had to attack Maiden Castle or if the inhabitants quietly accepted Roman dominion. Graves at the foot of the eastern entrance contain a number of people who died violent deaths but there is no evidence that they died at Maiden Castle or in AD 43. Is this a war grave from Vespasian's attack or a cemetery which developed over time?

After exploring the entrance continue along the south of the hillfort. The slope here is gentler than the north and four ramparts were built along this side. They snake out in front of you; four striking lines rising up and down in parallel until they turn to meet the western entrance.

BRONZE AGE VILLAGE
GRIMSPOUND, DEVON

Start King's Oven Car Park
Site Location SX701809,
OS 1:25,000 Explorer
map OL28, Dartmoor
Distance 5 miles
Time 2½ hours
Difficulty Moderate

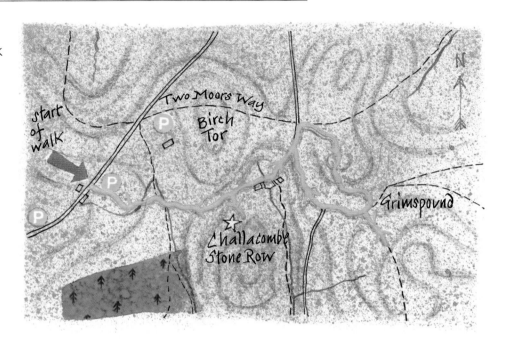

Dartmoor National Park is as famous for its prehistoric monuments and landscapes as for its ponies. Anyone wishing to walk on open moorland plateaux and explore ancient sites is spoiled for choice in an open access area where almost every footpath and bridleway passes within sight of a monument.

Dartmoor is perhaps best known for its reaves, stone rows and pounds. These are long-distance land boundaries, processional ways and enclosures most of which date from the late Neolithic to Bronze Age with the exception of some of the later pounds. There are also dozens of round houses, burial barrows and stone circles.

For me, one of the most interesting types of monument on Dartmoor is the pound and this walk will culminate in the most well known while taking in a stone row and some burials and hut circles. This walk will lead you via Challacombe Stone Row to view Grimspound in its landscape before entering through its original entrance. Challacombe was built during the late Neolithic or early Bronze Age between 2500 and 1500 BC while Grimspound was occupied a little more recently around 1000 BC.

The initial gentle climb along the bridleway through heather up to Headland Warren takes you through the remains of more recent activity on Dartmoor. The first things to catch the eye are the large gullies running across and alongside the bridleway. These are openworks or beams excavated between the medieval period and early twentieth century to mine tin ore in Dartmoor's richest mining district.

When you reach the ridge you gain your first view of Dartmoor's prehistoric past with monuments to the living and the dead visible in every direction. Approximately 400 metres (1,300 ft) along the ridge to your right are the stone-footed round houses of a settlement, while on the prominent Birch Tor up to your left is a burial mound. Looking straight ahead you will see a saddle of land hanging above a valley and between the distinctive Hookney and Hameldown Tors. This is Grimspound, and even at this distance you can make out the stone wall which encloses most of the gently sloping land between the tors.

Before we reach Grimspound, we pass the Challacombe Stone Row, which is half way down the valley side to the right of the footpath down towards the road ahead. By continuing to where the row starts close to the footpath, you can walk up hill along the row following a route prehistoric people would have trod approximately 4,000 years ago. The three parallel lines of stones that erupt from the coarse grass like shark's teeth are surprisingly small.

They were not designed to impress but simply to mark the way of a 160 metre (525 ft) ceremonial route through the landscape. To the south, the row ends in a wafer-thin triangular standing stone approximately 2 metres (6½ ft) high. To the north, where it ends at a stream, it points directly to the summit of Birch Tor and a burial mound dating from 4,500 and 3,500 years ago. The row was surely designed to lead

people to look or walk towards Birch Tor, which was clearly a significant landmark.

Our modern footpath cuts across this prehistoric avenue to cross a stream and run upslope towards Hookney Tor, where more stone footings of round houses lie scattered on the moorland to the north and east. Hookney is one of those distinctive Dartmoor tors which have a jumble of grey granite outcrops on their summits. At Hookney, the outcrops are wide flat-topped beds that look as though they are beginning to slip down through the heather into the valley.

They provide ideal viewing platforms for looking down into Grimspound, laid out below you as good as if seen in an aerial photograph, with Hambeldown Tor behind. It is easy to gain sight of Grimspound's

Dartmoor ponies graze above Grimspound, a Bronze Age enclosed settlement approximately 3,000 years old

Looking down on Grimspound with the Dartmoor landscape in the background

almost circular enclosure wall. within which lie the stone footings of twenty-four round houses. The original prehistoric entrance breaks the enclosure wall in the south-east on the opposite side of the settlement. The fields of the fertile valleys around Cator Court and Ponsworthy in the distance form a green triangle between the reds and russets of the closer moorlands.

Drop down from Hookney Tor, crossing the stream which would have supplied water to Grimspound,

and circle around the wall, built as two skins of large horizontally coursed slabs filled with rubble in between. Enter through the same gate the prehistoric occupants of the settlement used over 3,000 years ago, its massive granite slabs framing a view back towards Hookney Tor.

Once inside you can wander from one round house to another, even entering the doors of the best-preserved houses to stand inside homes which once thronged to the sounds and smells of family life. Sixteen

round houses were excavated in 1894, when porches, paved floors, hearths, possible stone benches, pottery, flints and cooking stones were discovered.

You can gain another good view of Grimspound from Hambeldown Tor before returning to the start of the walk. Either retrace your steps over Hookney Tor or follow the stream down from Grimspound to the road and then walk alongside Hookney Tor. Take the bridleway west to pass north of Birch Tor and it's a short distance down the road to the car park.

OVERLEAF *Walk through the original entrance into Grimspound to discover the remains of twenty-four prehistoric houses*

AT HOME IN THE IRON AGE
CHYSAUSTER, CORNWALL

Start Chysauster car
park
Site location
SW472350, OS
1:25,000 Explorer
map 102, Land's
End.
Length 3 miles
Time 2 hours
Difficulty Moderate
Family friendly

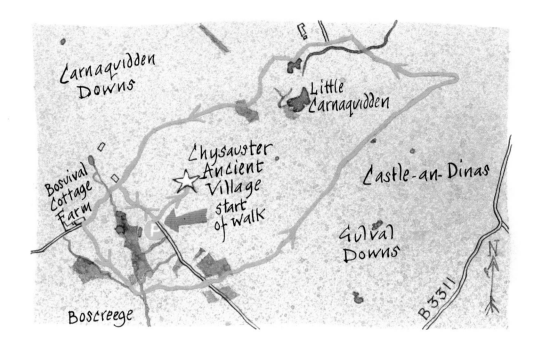

Chysauster ancient village is an Iron Age settlement where the walls of 2,000-year-old houses survive up to 3 metres (10 ft) high and you can still walk through original doorways to enter the rooms where Iron Age families cooked and slept.

Chysauster appears to have been occupied for approximately 100 years, or four generations, from its foundation a little before the Roman occupation of Britain. There are numerous villages from this period surviving on Cornwall's Lizard Peninsula and the Isles of Scilly, but Chysauster is the best preserved. This short walk takes in the traditional small fields of the West Penwith countryside around Chysauster, as well as a hillforts and burial mounds, before entering Chysauster's streets and houses.

Follow the road left out of the car park and around the corner for a short distance before taking the footpath on your left. The road is typical of West Penwith's narrow sunken lanes, tightly fastened in on both sides by high hedges. The footpath allows you to see the traditional walled hedge banks and small fields close up.

There is a group of particularly small and irregular

fields to the right; these are identical to those around Chysauster and may preserve the lines of boundaries dating back to the Iron Age. Small fields like these exist across much of West Penwith and suggest a densely populated landscape 2,000 years ago. The walk uphill and across the road passes prehistoric enclosures and round houses which may again be Iron Age, or even earlier, before coming on to the low summit of Tonkins Downs.

There are a number of early Bronze Age burial mounds on this locally high ground, as well as Castle-an-Dinas, where three concentric rings mark out a circular hillfort in what is now heath among quarries. The chronological relationship between the hillfort and Chysauster is unclear, so we cannot be sure whether the two were occupied simultaneously.

Beyond the hillfort the return to Chysauster meanders through gently rolling heath and walled and hedged farmland either side of a narrow wooded valley before slowly descending through similar countryside. Apart from the quarry, the landscape has probably changed little since the Iron Age. Most of the tree cover had been removed long before Chysauster was built. Some

of the fields may now be larger, and fertiliser-improved pastures may look a little more lush and green, but essentially the same intermingling existed then as does today of small fields for cereal crops and livestock, open heath for further grazing and woodlands.

The real delight in walking into prehistory at Chysauster is in exploring the village, because you can walk along a street, in and out of walled courtyards then enter rooms that were already part of a thriving settlement at the time Pompeii was buried beneath the hot ash and pumice which spewed from Mount Vesuvius in AD 79. But no volcanic eruption preserved these ancient buildings, nor the wind-blown sand which concealed Neolithic Skara Brae. The preservation of a small part of the original village is due solely to the strength built into the wide walls and the unpromising quality of the land which deterred later farmers.

Immediately upslope is rough heathland, while in all other directions lie fields created by combining and enlarging Chysauster's fields.

As you enter the site you wander up one of the village streets, passing between two of the more ruinous houses, to a triangular open area where the street turns sharply left. Level areas next to the houses were small gardens for growing vegetables and herbs.

Follow the Iron Age street towards a group of four houses nestled in close to each other. These are the best preserved of all the houses at Chysauster. Each has a main door leading off from the street so you can walk exactly in the steps of the Iron Age villagers.

It is only on entering that you realise how complicated these houses really are, for you are faced with a series of doors leading into three or more individual rooms. Imagine each building as a cluster of small oval rooms

Chysauster is a 2,000-year-old village where today, you can still wander along streets, and into courtyards and houses.

The hollowed stone may have supported a timber hinge for a wooden door in the nearby entrance between courtyard and room.

or houses sharing the same outer walls around a central courtyard. What are now turfed walls supported conical thatched roofs. The courtyard is bustling with people working, maybe sharpening farming tools, cooking meals or weaving, depending on the weather. The people moving about are all part of an extended family of possibly ten or more relatives, including parents, brothers, sisters, children, aunts, uncles and cousins.

The size of the oval house at the far end of the courtyard, opposite where you have entered, suggests this is where the head of the household lives. This is the largest room, measuring about 7 × 3.5 metres (24 × 12 ft), and most objects were discovered here during excavations. Smaller rooms to either side of the courtyard may have been occupied by other members of the family and used for storage. The courtyard and rooms were paved and the wooden entrance doors swung open and shut on a pole-hinge resting in the hollow of a floor-stone. Look out for stone-lined narrow channels built into the floors. These brought clean water into the houses and carried the dirty water out.

Inside one of Chysauster's courtyards looking trough the door into the main room.

We do not know why Chysauster was abandoned but there is no evidence for a violent or sudden end as at Pompeii or Skara Brae, nor that the climate was appreciably worsening. It may be that the population moved elsewhere as they exhausted local soils or simply that times changed and families no longer felt the need or desire to live so close to each other in villages. Whatever the reason, the community who worked, slept, laughed, shouted and cried in this village have left us with an enduring monument to their lives.

MONARCH OF ALL IT SURVEYS
BRITISH CAMP, MALVERN HILLS

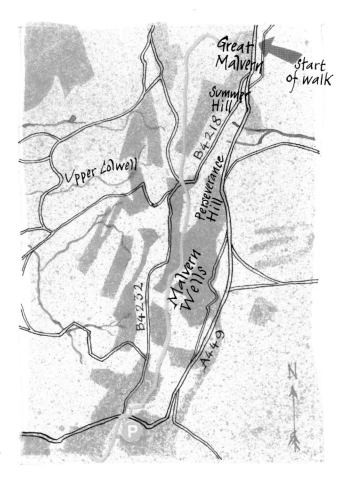

The Malvern Hills form a spine of grassy peaks fringed with trees which run north to south through Herefordshire and Worcestershire. They are celebrated walking country and home to two Iron Age hillforts, with British Camp on Herefordshire Beacon being one of England's most visually dramatic eyries.

While British Camp can be explored from a car park near its base, the best way to understand why this site was chosen for the hillfort over 2,000 years ago is to walk the high route along the top of the Malverns from Great Malvern. The hillfort appears and disappears as you approach, a banded grassy peak standing out from the wooded slopes before finally revealing itself as a majestic hilltop citadel.

Begin by leaving Great Malvern on the footpath to St Anne's Well and once there take the path up to Worcestershire Beacon from the multitude of routes available. Open grassland dominates the Malvern ridge, and soon you will glimpse a distinctive grassy mound standing to one side of the main line of peaks. It is reminiscent of an ancient Babylonian ziggurat, as alternating rings of ramparts and ditches give a stepped profile to slopes below the flat-topped summit. The stone-and-earth ramparts are still impressive despite two millennia which have softened their lines and lowered their contours.

Imagine how much more imposing they looked when freshly constructed, the thick walls of dark granite and shady ditches forming shadowy stripes around the contours of the otherwise natural slopes. What an awe-inspiring monument to impress strangers, while the resident population would have been assured of their safety and convinced of their

Start Great Malvern
Site location SO759400, OS 1:25,000
   Explorer map 190, Malvern Hills and
   Bredon Hill
Distance 8½ miles
Time 5 hours
Difficulty Difficult

own importance. The ramparts not only defended the people who lived there, but also embellished the natural slopes, turning the hill from part of the natural landscape into a cultural, inhabited place.

The hillfort was built in at least two phases. First came an enclosure around the top of Herefordshire Beacon, thought to have been begun about 200 BC. Later in the Iron Age, the ramparts were extended along lower shoulders of land to the north and south of the original hillfort.

Our approach to the hillfort takes us down from Black Hill, across Wynds Point, then up towards one of the entrances from the car park. Here there are two choices; you can follow the upper track through the north-east entrance of the second phase of ramparts then straight over the rampart of the earliest hillfort, where it diverges from the prehistoric route, which took a curving course to the left to double-back in through the Iron Age entrance. Alternatively, you could take the gentler lower track, which follows the contour of the hill, then climb up along the narrow path beside a wooden seat to come to one of the major entrances buried in the waist of the hillfort. The footpath allows you to enter via what was a gate created by overlapping the walls, so that you have to walk closely below a rampart before you gain entry.

The effect is much the same today as it was over 2,000 years ago. You see the defended bulk of Herefordshire Beacon rise steeply above you. The climb on to the top of the Beacon is a strenuous short uphill burst, one that can leave you breathless. When you reach the top you climb on to a final artificial

British Camp occupies a commanding position in the Malverns

mound, known as the Citadel, though this is a mere 1,000 years old and the remains of a medieval castle built by the Normans who quickly identified the defensive potential of the long-abandoned hillfort.

The views, as along most of the walk, take in miles of country to the east, west and south, demonstrating the commanding position the Malverns offered to Iron Age communities. To the west lies the low jumble of Herefordshire's wooded hills running into the Welsh Marches; to the east is Worcestershire, where the River Severn plain stretches out flat and uninterrupted as far as the hazy Cotswolds on the horizon. The modern towns of Tewkesbury and Gloucester, and fields of rolling farmland are laid out far below you.

The Malverns form a chain of abrupt peaks to north and south, their tree-cloaked slopes beautiful at any time of year but particularly magnificent in autumn. The overwhelming feeling is of being on top of the world, the monarch of all you survey. The

Iron Age community could have chosen almost any Malvern peak to build a hillfort, and indeed another community built a similar hillfort on Midsummer Hill 2.5 km (1½ miles) to the south. A hillfort on any of the Malvern Hills would advertise the community's presence to its neighbours and give that community the security of living on high.

British Camp has no water source. This fact, along with its exposed position, begs the question as to whether people ever lived here all year round. In fact, this is a question which can be posed about many hillforts. Faint round house platforms have been seen inside the hillfort, suggesting a sizeable population who would have needed to trek downhill for water every day. Our modern expectations of what is uncomfortably exposed and how far we will travel for water may be very different to those of Iron Age people – something to ponder on as you walk back north along the Malvern ridge to the comforts of Great Malvern.

Looking west over one of British Camp's ramparts towards the Herefordshire hills

WALES

SKELETON OF A TOMB
PENTRE IFAN, PEMBROKESHIRE

The skeletal, originally earth-covered, stone tomb at Pentre Ifan is the largest and best-preserved Neolithic dolmen in Britain. It is also one of the most graceful dolmens, a type of chambered tomb where a large capstone is supported on thin stone pillars which make it appear as if it is suspended in the air. This tomb was built on the edge of the Preseli Mountains in approximately 3500 BC, with views for miles across the Nevern Valley to Cardigan Bay.

Follow the bridleway through the Pentre Ifan nature reserve, an oak-dominated native broadleaved woodland, to gain an idea of what the Neolithic landscape surrounding the burial chamber would have been like. There are a number of small clearings and plenty of boggy ground. Families would have lived in timber houses in clearings or the edge of woodland, pasturing their livestock and growing crops on the more open ground. The chamber would have been built in a larger open area so that

Pentre Ifan is one of Wales' most famous prehistoric monuments

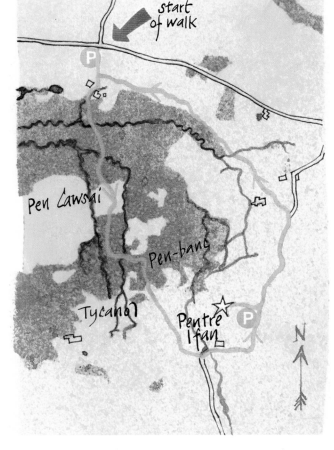

Start Pentre Ifan nature reserve car park, south of Nevern

Site location SN099370, OS 1:25,000 Explorer map OL35, North Pembrokeshire

Distance 2 miles

Time 1 hour

Difficulty Moderate

Accessible

these families could see it, and so they could see their homes when gathering for ceremonies around the mound.

Turn left when you reach the lane and look out for your first sight of the dolmen on your left past trees and over fields that may have cattle. Apart from the regimented rows of conifers in the background, this scene isn't too far removed from the view Neolithic people would have had of the completed mound. The lane takes you around to the entrance to the dolmen, which is from the east and unlikely to be on the line of a formal Neolithic route to the chamber. To get an idea of how the original mound would have been experienced in the Neolithic period, head around to the southern end of the dolmen.

Today the dolmen is a graceful arrangement of upright blue stones, three of which balance the

beautifully proportioned wedge-shaped capstone on their upright points. The capstone has a remarkably light and airy feel for a stone estimated to weigh 16 tonnes. During the Neolithic period, a mound surrounded the dolmen, though it is unclear whether it covered all but the top of the capstone or just formed a low platform around the base of the supporting stones. The outline of the mound can still be seen on the ground; it was 36 metres (18 ft) long.

The dolmen was at the southern end of the mound and created a chamber with a stone façade facing south. Five of stones from the façade survive upright; others are fallen around them. The stone mound would have continued beyond the façade to form two curving horns which created a ceremonial space with the mound as backdrop. One of the upright stones in the façade is a false door, which may have been moved

A view of Pentre Ifan from the south-west shows its location above the Nevern Valley

to allow worshippers to enter the chamber where the bones of ancestors were placed.

Neolithic religious leaders would have conducted ancestral ceremonies in front of this façade, watched by the community who could see the Nevern Valley, Dinas Head and the Irish Sea beyond. Symbolic and social links between the gods, the dead and the land were probably created during these ceremonies.

The rugged Preseli Mountains ring the dolmen to the west and south where distinctive outcrops of bluestone punctuate the heathland. These mountains are famously the source of the bluestones used to build the earliest phase of Stonehenge at about the same time Pentre Ifan was built. The intriguing question is – what was the connection between the builders of Stonehenge and the communities of Pentre Ifan? You may not discover the answer on the return to your starting point, found by continuing along the lane and taking the footpath to the left, but you will gain a strong sense of the wooded landscape Neolithic people moved through to reach Pentre Ifan.

LEFT *Pentre Ifan's capstone is balanced on the points of three upright stones*

ABOVE *The view of the dolmen from this angle captures its form but would have been impossible in the Neolithic when the mound covered the chamber*

CROWN OF BLUESTONE
FOEL DRYGARN, PEMBROKESHIRE

Start Car park north-west
of Mynachlog-ddu
Site location SN158336,
OS 1:25,000 Explorer
map OL35, North
Pembrokeshire
Distance 11 miles
Time 5 hours
Difficulty Difficult

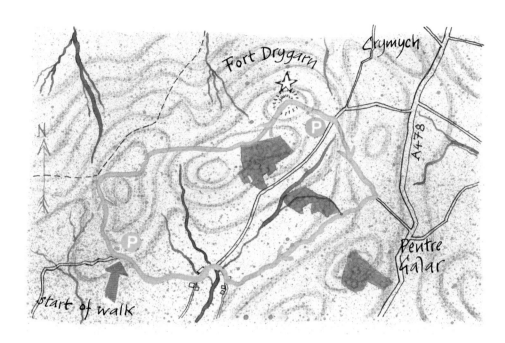

*Foel Drygarn hillfort is at the end of a
ridge in the Preseli Mountains, famous
as the source of Stonehenge's bluestone
circle*

Foel Drygarn is Pembrokeshire's most spectacular Iron Age hillfort, enclosing a dome-shaped hill which forms the north-western end of a ridge punctuated by dramatic outcrops of tumbling boulders and fractured rock. The hill is topped with a row of three large Bronze Age cairns and offers spectacular views of the Irish Sea and Welsh mountains.

The hillfort is in the Preseli Mountains, made famous as the source of the bluestone for Stonehenge. A possible quarry from where some of the stones may have been taken is on the route to Foel Drygarn.

Begin along the bridleway from the car park north-west of Mynachlog-ddu and climb through walled pastures on to the Preselis west of Craig Tailfyndd. This hill is like much of the Preseli range, a low summit at the top of a steep incline mottled yellow and brown with rough grassland and heather. There is a haunting air about the Preselis, brought about from the abrupt openness of the land and the slightly washed-out appearance of the vegetation, which is transformed during late summer when the heather comes into bloom and the hills are brought to life with a carpet of vivid purple.

At the top of the ridge you have your first views north and west to Cardigan Bay and an old drovers' road where for centuries cattle were taken to market.

Turning right on to this route you climb on to the sloping summit between Carn Bica and Carn Siân. You are now right in the middle of the strange Preseli landscape, where open land cascades down towards distant fields and steel-cold outcrops erupt out of summits and higher slopes. Jumbled rows and mounds of bluestone appear to have been pushed up and out of the ground where they have fractured and tumbled apart. Each outcrop has its own distinctive personality profiled against the sky; Carn Siân is a triumphal statue; Carn Bica, a grey pyramid.

These outcrops attracted Neolithic people from the surrounding area who copied the natural geology by building mounds to bury their dead around them. Carn Bica has a small burial cairn at its base and near by is a small curving alignment of stones known as Bedd Arthur, which looks prehistoric though its date is yet to be proved. Though small it has attracted an Arthurian legend, and it is said to be one of the resting places of Arthur's father, Uther Pendragon, as well as a story that it was thrown here from Dyffryn stone circle, over 8 miles to the south-west.

The drovers' road continues east, passing to the north of Carn Menyn, where a large Neolithic chambered tomb can be found at the head of the natural band of rocks tumbling down the slope known

The bulk of Foel Drygarn seems to gather itself from the north to finish in a dramatic rocky finale to the south

as Stone River. The tomb has partly collapsed down the slope below the small summit it is built up on and its most striking feature is the large flat capstone of a chamber lying at a discarded angle in the centre of the mound. There is something desolate about the way this ruinous mound lies abandoned in the bleak grassland below Carn Menyn.

Menyn is one of the largest outcrops in this area: a tortured battlement of pillars and jagged spikes fashioned from split and angled dolerite. This is one of the possible sources of Stonehenge's bluestones, and archaeologists have been searching for the quarry that provided the actual standing stones. The attraction of the place as a Neolithic quarry is obvious: so many of the pillars look like standing stones just waiting to be levered out of place and on to wooden rollers to begin their 250 km (155 mile) journey by land, sea and river to Salisbury Plain.

north and east are striped bands of grass and rock dropping down from the summit. It is only when you are at the base of the hill itself that you can make out parts of the three bands of rocks that form the collapsed ramparts encircling the hill.

The wind always seems to pick up when you reach the summit, but you can find shelter between the three huge cairns aligned from south-west to north-east. They stand up to 3 metres (10 ft) high and give the hillfort its name – Foel Drygarn being Welsh for Hill of the Three Cairns. The cairns are burial mounds dating from the end of the Neolithic or the beginning of the Bronze Age, approximately 4,500 years ago, and mark the sites individuals considered important enough to be commemorated on top of such a prominent hill.

The hillfort was built at least 1,500 years later by a community who thought the hill and its three burials a very important site and left the cairns untouched while seeking the stone needed to build the ramparts. Many Iron Age hillforts were built on hills used for earlier burials, including Mam Tor and Tre'r Ceiri to name but two, by communities who wanted to attract social status by living on and controlling sacred hills. Traces of nearly 270 house platforms survive on the hill, though most are easier to see from the air than on the ground. In 1899, excavations of some of the house platforms found Iron Age and Romano-British pottery, spindle whorls for spinning wool, glass beads, jet rings and sling shots.

The views from Foel Drygarn take in a vast sweep of south-west Wales. You can look back along your route over the Preseli Mountains as well as the Cambrian Mountains to the north and the Brecon Beacons to the east. The Preseli seem to flow downwards until they reach the farmland and woodlands below. Pentre Ifan is only a short distance to the north-west, beyond which are wooded valleys then the shimmering Irish Sea.

The descent from Foel Drygarn is steep and quick and takes you past Mountain-bach Farm towards Crug-yr-hwch chambered tomb. From here you can either return to Mynachlog-ddu along the road or continue on a footpath across the road to pick up a quiet lane to the village via Dolaumaen, where you can take a diversion to a group of standing stones.

However, evidence of dates and quarry activity have still to be found.

The route from Carn Menyn to Foel Drygarn passes more fantastical outcrops and the occasional prehistoric burial mound. The hillfort looms ever closer, a gentle round profile upslope from the left until abruptly cleaved through to reveal a series of serrated bluestone outcrops. Heather cloaks the southern side in a red-brown mantle, while the

BRONZE AGE SUN BURST
BRYN CADER FANER, GWYNEDD

Start Car park at end
of the road east of
Eisingrug

Site location
SH648353. OS
1:25,000 Explorer
map OL18, Harlech,
Porthmadog & Bala

Distance 4 miles

Time 2 hours

Difficulty Difficult

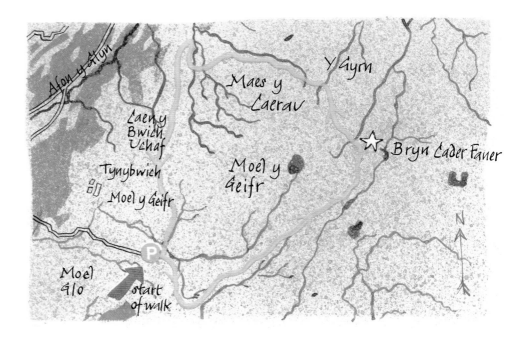

There is possibly no more intriguing prehistoric monument in Britain or Ireland than the cairn of Bryn Cader Faner, a stone mound with thin slabs projecting at an angle from its base like the rays of the sun or a crown of thorns. No other site looks like it or provides the same eerie effect when you reach it, across boggy moorland surrounded by the Cambrian Mountains. It is a rewarding discovery at the end of a long walk, with some superb views across Cardigan Bay and much of Snowdonia National Park.

Finding the small car park at the start of the footpath can be quite a trial in itself, as it is hidden away at the end of narrow roads winding up the mountainside from the Portmerion to Harlech road. Once on the path, you follow a water company track before heading off across bouncy moorland peat along a small hanging valley between the craggy peaks of some of southern Snowdonia's dramatic mountains.

They rise in a series of damp ledges and rocky edges up to the western heights of Moel Ysgyfarnogod, 623

metres (2,043 ft) above sea level, a swirling mass of stone and peat in the centre of a wall-like ridge, which luckily keeps its most fearsome side to the east. The footpath follows a natural routeway between high lakes formed where streams cascade down the slopes into the hollows of the hanging valley.

There seems little reason for anyone in prehistory to spend much time at these altitudes, unless perhaps hunting deer or herding sheep during the summer. Yet you pass by the occasional Bronze Age burial cairn and then the faint shadows of round houses preserved as low circles of stones, so it is clear that people did live up here during prehistory. As there is no sign of field systems it is likely that only some members of a family came here during part of the year, probably to look after sheep.

Whoever stayed here knew that enough people visited to make it worth the effort of constructing an elaborate and striking burial mound on a knoll where it would be silhouetted against the sky. Yet if you walk towards the area from the north it is easy not to see the cairn, as its position on the south of the knoll shields it from view. Clearly the people who built the monument expected many others to see it, but only when approaching from the south. The prehistoric route from the south follows much the same line as today's footpath and minor roads up from the coast, only 5 km (3 miles) to the west.

You first see Bryn Cader Faner as you round a small promontory and spot the thin slabs of stone erupting from the ground against the skyline to the north-west, where the end of the hanging valley rises up to create a false horizon. It is so perfectly placed that you do not lose sight of it again if you climb the knoll directly towards it.

Close up, it is a stone mound 8.5 metres (28 ft) across and less than 1 metre (3 ft) high, from the body of which projects a ring of fifteen 2 metre (6½ ft) long slabs, all angled outwards to create the crown or sun ray effect. There used to be thirty projecting stones but the army removed half of them during manoeuvres before the Second World War, when they used the cairn for target practice. Bryn Cader Faner has not been dated but it is most likely early Bronze Age, dating from some time between 2500 and 1500 BC.

From the cairn, you can see south-west to the coast just beyond Harlech and north across the Vale of Ffestiniog to the heart of the Cambrian Mountains around Blaenau Ffestiniog right over to Snowdon. Some archaeologists have suggested that the prehistoric track passing Bryn Cader Faner is part of a long-distance gold route running west to east from Ireland by way of a port at Llanbedr and to south-west England via Trawsfynydd, Bala and the Tanat Valley. But it would seem a lot easier to carry on sailing down the coast and along the Severn Estuary than to haul your gold over the precipitous mountains of central Wales. Bryn Cader Faner would have been a monumental marker on what was, perhaps, more local east to west movement in the Welsh valleys and to the coast.

We will divert from this possible prehistoric route to return towards the coast via the rough farmland below Moel y Geifr, passing a small group of less ornate prehistoric cairns at the point with a view across Traeth Bach to Porthmadog and the mountains beyond.

From here the land tumbles down in a series of

narrow valleys and ridges enclosed with dark dry-stone walls into small fields and strips of deciduous woodland. Abandoned farmsteads of many ages litter the ground – bone-hard where the bedrock forms sheer plates running with water from mountain springs and boggy where the water collects behind other outcrops. Any useful soils between these two extremes are thin and good only for sheep-farming. The footpath picks a way south along the contour to return to the car park via Moel-y-geifr farm.

ABOVE *The dramatic slabs of Bryn Cader Faner projecting from the body of the cairn, with views to Snowdonia to the north-west*

BELOW *Bryn Cader Faner is perfectly placed in the landscape to catch your eye as your approach it from the south, along the line of a possible prehistoric route linking Ireland, Wales and England*

CITADEL IN THE CLOUDS
TRE'R CEIRI, GWYNEDD

Start Llithfaen

Site location
SH373446, OS
1:25,000 Explorer map
254, Lleyn Peninsula,
East

Distance 4 miles

Time 3 hours

Difficulty Difficult

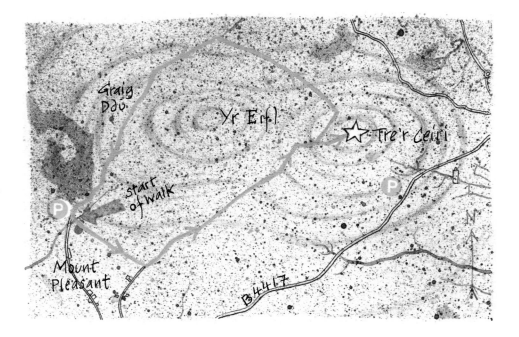

Tre'r Ceiri is the most impressive hillfort in Wales, possibly in the whole of Britain. One of the desolate, rocky peaks of Yr Eifl is ringed with massive stone ramparts at 450 metres (1,476 ft) above sea level which enclose clusters of stone-walled round houses. This is truly a citadel in the clouds, and when the clouds lift, the views across Wales and the Irish Sea are spellbinding.

The best approach to Tre'r Ceiri is along the Llŷn Peninsula Coastal Path, beginning at Porth-y-Nant car park north-west near Llithfaen to the south-west, where impressive views of the flat-topped mountain are gained. The hillfort plays hide-and-seek behind the lower plateau to begin with, while its higher neighbour to the west stands proud.

When you reach the low plateau between the rocky knoll of Caergribin on your right and the tallest peak of Yr Eifl on your left, you see Tre'r Ceiri in its full splendour. The mountain rises gracefully out of a sea of heather and bracken washing around its base, its gently curving flanks mottled with grey scree. Its summit appears almost flat, when not shrouded in cloud, and beckons you to climb on up to it among the crows who soar and dive on updraughts above the ramparts.

The path takes you directly towards the mountain and as you get closer look out for the nick on the summit's skyline which gives away the location of the west-facing entrance. The Llŷn Coastal Path climbs up a natural break in the slope and may follow the approximate line of an Iron Age route to the hillfort, though we don't know if there was a dedicated path up to the entrance or whether people climbed up to the hillfort across open ground from all directions. The wide plateau was probably part of the hillfort's farmland, a mixture of pasture for sheep and cattle along with small fields of barley or oats. As the climate cooled and became wetter during the Iron Age, it would have become harder to grow crops on these soils, and the land would all have been given over to rough grazing as coarse grasses and heather took hold.

When you reach the base of Tre'r Ceiri proper you get a real sense of how hillforts offered such good security to those who lived in them. The walk from here is steep and arduous, and the higher you climb the

more difficult it gets to clamber over the loose rock of the scree which is damp almost all year round. There would be little chance for a small group of people to make any sort of raid on the inhabitants of Tre'r Ceiri. The entrance is built right on the scree, though much of the rock around it is probably collapsed ramparts, making progress even more difficult. As you finally stumble through the long stone-walled entrance, the prospect of the flatter grass beyond is a tempting reward for your effort.

There is little to see at first glance from just inside the entrance, but as you move further into the hillfort's interior the full scale of the site and the sheer effort it must have taken to build it are revealed. Bear right and you will soon see what remains of the mighty stone rampart.

Even after 2,000 years of collapse it is a magnificent sight. Rocks are tight-packed to form a wall nearly 2 metres (6½ ft) wide and over 1 metre (3¼ ft) high, which snakes along the break of slope where the steep mountainsides meet the flatter summit. The wall is magnificently atmospheric when mist curls around the mountain to hide and reveal the ramparts time and again, alternately cloaking them in shadow then exposing them to sunlight.

The ground keeps rising as you continue into the hillfort's interior, fractured knolls adding punctuation marks to the line of the rampart, until the eastern end rushes skywards in a flank of ground buried deep in grey scree and crowns the hillfort with a rounded summit. Look closely at the more level ground below this scree and you will see that some of the stones form a connected pattern of grey circles and ovals among the heather which spreads from the ramparts on one side of the hillfort to the other. These are some of the round houses where Tre'r Ceiri's former inhabitants lived.

You can still wander in and out of the remains of these Iron Age homes through narrow gaps where wooden doors once kept out the cold winds and rain. Tumbled house walls stand between ankle and waist high, some not much lower than when they were first built. The walls supported the lower ends of wooden rafters made from young tree trunks which came together at an apex above the centre of the house. A thick roof of heather, bracken or straw sat on the rafters. Where today you see rings of stone open to the sky, 2,000 years ago these would have been dark rooms filled with smoke and warmth from central hearths. The air would have been pungent with smoke, cooked food and sweat.

You really appreciate the scale of the hillfort and its houses when you climb on to the top of the rocky summit and look south-west along the interior. Clear days give views right down the Llŷn Peninsula,

east to Snowdonia, south down the Welsh coast, north to Anglesey and west to the Irish Sea either side of Yr Eifl. But Tre'r Ceiri is always subject to the weather, and the summit is often windy and cloaked in mist.

Drop down from the summit to the western rampart and follow this back to the entrance. When you reach the base of Tre'r Ceiri you can once more pick up the Llŷn Coastal Path as it skirts the northern flank of the site.

Follow this north-west and Tre'r Ceiri will disappear behind the bulk of Yr Eifl while views across the Irish Sea to Anglesey will open up before you drop down into Nant Gwrtheyrn valley. The valley is named after Vortigern, the King of the Britons who exiled King Arthur's father Uther Pendragon and, according to one legend, is said to have lived here. Turn south to return to the car park.

The view down the Llŷn Peninsula from the top of Tre'r Ceiri's ramparts

EAR TO THE GROUND
BRYN CELLI DDU, ANGLESEY

Start Bryn Celli Ddu car
park.

Site location
SH50757017, OS
1:25,000 Explorer map
263, Anglesey East

Length 1 mile

Time 1 hour

Difficulty Easy

Family friendly

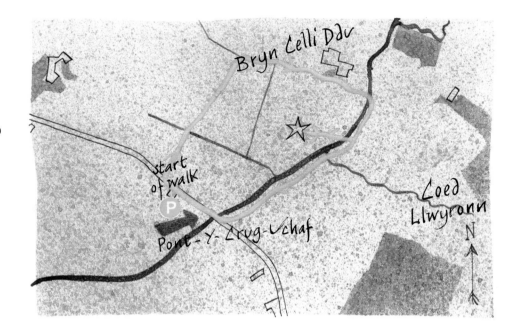

Sunrise over Snowdonia. Bryn Celli Ddu is one of Anglesey's best-known and most evocative Neolithic chambered tombs

Anglesey is famed for the number of Neolithic chambered tombs found lurking in field corners and beside walls across the island. Barcolidiad y Gawres, Bodowyr, Plas Newydd, Presaddfed, Trefignath and Ty Newydd are just some of the stone burial chambers which attract visitors to the island.

These ancestral mounds were built approximately 5,000 years ago to house the bones of the dead in distinctive landmarks which would be visible to people living and working in the surrounding landscapes. The difficulty is in choosing one tomb to represent the whole of Anglesey, an even more onerous task knowing that people interested in archaeology who have visited the island all have their favourite. I've chosen Bryn Celli Ddu, the 'mound in the dark grove', partly because it's my favourite, partly because of its fascinating development from henge to tomb, and not

least because you can enjoy a short family-friendly circuit around it to experience the visual presence of burial chambers in the Anglesey landscape.

If you start at the nearby car park, turn left along the road rather than right and take the first footpath on your right. Follow this farm track right around to walk a short circuit which will bring you to Bryn Celli Ddu after the farm of the same name. This is a good way to appreciate the location chosen by the local Neolithic farming community to build what was first a henge then a communal tomb inside a mound.

Bryn Celli Ddu is on a slight rise in gently rolling lowland farmland, which makes it a prominent landmark for the whole of the walk and a few miles beyond. Today, it is surrounded by improved pastures for cattle and sheep, hedgerows and small conifer plantations.

The forecourt and entrance to the passage inside Bryn Celli Ddu. An ox was buried outside the entrance

Strip away this well-managed, neat landscape to imagine a land that was similarly open in nature but less ordered. There would have been grazing for livestock, though the grass wouldn't have been quite so lush and green, intermingled with groves of natural mixed deciduous woodland. The edges between the two wouldn't have been quite as clearly demarcated as today, though the mound would have been in an open location so it could be seen. A tall single standing stone visible on the ridge to the left of the track is likely to date from the Bronze Age, maybe 500 or 1,000 years after Bryn Celli Ddu was built, showing how important this landscape remained for later generations.

It is just before the farm that a Neolithic ceremonial approach is likely to have been oriented on the mound, running towards the north-east-facing entrance to the chamber. We are prevented from following this line by a private field, so have to continue to circumnavigate the mound by beginning a gentle descent into a valley, the other side of which is a long run of conifers, before turning south to pick up the modern footpath to Bryn Celli Ddu. Beyond the conifers the landscape takes a more dramatic turn, as the peaks of Snowdonia form a distant jagged horizon to the east.

Bryn Celli Ddu is more than a single monument. In about 3000 BC it began life as a henge almost 35 metres (115 ft) in diameter, which enclosed a circular area containing a stone circle of fourteen stones. A stone decorated with cup marks was erected near the centre next to a pit in which a fire was lit then a human ear bone was placed on the cooling ground and covered by a stone slab. This elaborate and somewhat strange ritual may have prepared the ground for the building of the chambered tomb, though whether the ear bone symbolised something about communicating with the gods or dead, or had some other meaning altogether we may never know.

What is unusual in Wales is the henge itself – a rare Neolithic monument in this part of Britain. This may show that the builders and worshippers of Bryn Celli Ddu were networked in to wider social relationships which perhaps brought them and communities to the east in contact with each other.

Soon after the henge was built the stone circle was taken down and a mound built to cover a burial chamber and a cup-marked standing stone, which was the only stone retained from the circle. Today, a replica marks its location while the original stone is in the National Museum of Wales in Cardiff. Today's mound was rebuilt after excavation in 1928 and is quite a bit smaller than the Neolithic one.

Walk around to the fence opposite the entrance facing towards the farm to look at the chamber as Neolithic people attending ceremonies would have done. A jagged row of white limestone kerb stones creates a backdrop to a forecourt in front of the entrance which was defined by an area of quartz pebbles and hearths. A rectangular area in front of this, marked on three sides by rows of stones, some of which you can still see, was the scene of an ox burial. The entrance faces the midwinter sunrise, putting Bryn Celli Ddu on a par with Newgrange and Maes Howe.

You can still enter the passage by squeezing between two large portal stones and walking crouched along the stone-lined passage, a dry tunnel of straight-faced boulders which support a stone roof. There is enough space and natural light to follow the passage easily to the underground chamber framed by another two portal stones. Light shines in from the slit in the end of the chamber ahead as well as from the entrance.

The chamber walls are built from massive flat-faced dark stone slabs which support two large capstones. A rounded pillar lurks in the shadows beside one of the portal stones, a rare feature in chambered tombs, and which was probably the focus for rituals. It was in the chamber that communal burials were made, selected bones from the dead placed with each other in ceremonies that celebrated the ancestral origins of the community as well as the continuing presence of the departed in the world of the living.

Eventually the entrance to the passage was blocked with a mixture of stones, earth and bones so that people could no longer enter the chamber. Many chambered tombs were sealed later in the Neolithic or during the Bronze Age and may have been a sign that the power of the ancestors had subsided as new religions took hold.

And just maybe, as this chambered tomb was built, used for ceremonies, blocked, fell out of use, and was named by Welsh speakers and revisited by tourists, the ear bone left in the ground by the henge builders listened to all the generations who followed.

OPPOSITE *Looking along Bryn Celli Ddu's stone-lined passage from the entrance with the burial chamber illuminated by natural light at the far end*

IRELAND

TOMBS OF THE DECORATED STONES
NEWGRANGE, KNOWTH AND DOWTH (BRÚ NA BÓINNE), CO. MEATH

Start Brú na Bóinne
 Visitors Centre
Site location
 O0068972741, OSI
 1:50,000 Discovery
 Map D43, Dublin,
 Louth, Meath
Distance 1 mile
Time 2 hours
Difficulty Easy
Accessible

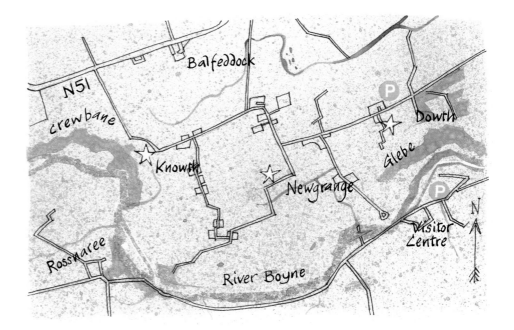

Newgrange passage tomb is one of the largest prehistoric tombs in Europe

There are few other places in the world that match the mystique of Newgrange and the winter solstice dawn sunlight that slowly creeps along the passage until it illuminates the chamber deep inside the mound. The spectacle, which lasts only seventeen minutes, is a match for similar solar events at the Pyramids and Stonehenge, both of which Newgrange pre-dates.

Newgrange is one of more than forty massive passage tombs built to be temples as much as graves at the Bend in the Boyne over 5,000 years ago. The monuments which cluster on the northern bank of the River Boyne were built by people who were well connected throughout this part of Ireland, people who could galvanise huge populations to build massive mounds from stones collected from river cobbles, greywacke slate, sandstone slabs, sea-rolled granite and gleaming quartz.

The stones show how far the regional relationships of Newgrange's builders reached, for while the cobbles came from the nearby river and the large kerb stones were brought from a few kilometres to the north, the quartz came from the Wicklow Mountains 40 km (25 miles) to the south and the granite from Dundalk Bay 35 km (21 miles) further north.

As at Avebury and Stonehenge, Newgrange was important to people living across a large area and the river was essential to transport the thousands of tonnes of rocks needed for the monuments, in a time when there were no wheels or horses in Ireland. The river would have been more than just a convenient transport route. It would have held a more spiritual place in this sacred landscape and so that is where our journey begins.

Today, visitors can only visit Newgrange and Knowth by bus from the Brú na Bóinne Visitor Centre situated on the opposite bank of the Boyne. The bus takes you along narrow hedged lanes that meander through rolling pastures and the occasional arable fields circumnavigating Newgrange en route, so that your first glimpse of the massive mound 76 metres (250 ft) across and 12 metres (40 ft) high, is from the side. Modern management has cut off both monuments from their landscapes.

As at Stonehenge, demands of conservation and

visitor management have created intensively-designed contemporary landscapes to manage access to the monuments, so preventing visitors from approaching the sites along their prehistoric routes or experiencing them in any way that prehistoric people did. This is also evident at Newgrange and Knowth, where ambitious rebuilding programmes have created mounds which

TOP *One of the 40 Neolithic passage tombs along the River Boyne*

ABOVE *Visitors queue to enter the passage deep inside Newgrange* may bear little resemblance to their original forms.

When you get off the bus and are ushered to the reception building, take time to look up at the dramatic reconstructed quartz pebble entrance and think of arriving here by foot from the valley you can see below you. It is down where the river flows that the Neolithic people of the Boyne would have processed up to the temple tombs, probably through a landscape of woodlands, open pastures and small plots of cereals.

The hundreds or thousands of Neolithic builders of the Brú na Bóinne temple tombs carried most of the boulders and stones from the river bank. They would have found it a long and arduous task; the rocks of Newgrange alone total over 250,000 tonnes. There was no let up in the hard labour for perhaps fifty years or more at each of the sites of Newgrange, Knowth and Dowth. When the communities used the temple tombs for worship, they probably retraced the steps of the builders from river to hilltop monument.

Each massive mound is penetrated by stone-lined passages, but you can only enter the one in Newgrange. There are two at Knowth, facing east and west, which almost meet in the centre of the mound. Neolithic worshippers at Newgrange had to climb over the huge decorated stone in front of the entrance, but there are steps around this for today's visitor.

Look up to the square opening above the door, known as the light box. As you squeeze into the narrow passage now lit with electricity, think of Neolithic people beginning the final part of a spiritual journey into the dark underground world of ancestors and spirits. Their only light would have been tallow candles or tree bark torches that filled the small space with thick smoke. You can easily see the elaborately carved symbols and grooves which Neolithic people would have glimpsed in flickering candlelight or felt in the pitch black.

The prehistoric journey ends 19 metres (60 ft) deep inside the mound, where three chambers forming a cross housed the bones of revered ancestors. These massive monuments were not graves as we think of them, but temples, where selected defleshed body parts of the dead were used in ceremonies, possibly before burial elsewhere.

There is so much to take in at the chambers, which are decorated with spirals, lozenges and lines pecked into the rock. A polished stone 'pillow' on the floor of

each chamber was probably an altar. Above you the corbelled roof uses flat stones balanced on top of each other to hold up the massive weight of rock and earth that continues for at least 5 metres (16 ft) above the roof.

If you are lucky enough to win the annual Newgrange solstice lottery, you can be inside the far end of the passage when the sunlight of the winter solstice sunrise gradually slides along the floor of the passage

to reach right into the chambers with a bright, rich orange intensity. It enters through the light box that was above your head at the entrance. The builders of Newgrange inclined the passage up so that the floor at the far end is the same height as the light box.

After Newgrange you can get back on the bus to Knowth, about 2 km (1¼ miles) to the north-west. The modern entrance from the road is just to the north of the chambered tomb and unlikely to be on an original prehistoric route. For the 1,000 or so years that Knowth was used as a temple it would have also been approached from the Boyne to the south-east.

Knowth is heavily rebuilt to give a feel of how it might have looked 5,000 years ago with grass-topped satellite tombs encircling the massive central mound. What you see today reconstructed is based on excavations that discovered the two stone-lined passages lying deep inside the mound and the

Knowth passage tomb with its kerb of large, carved kerb stones and some of its satellite tombs

impressive rock art carved on over 200 kerb stones that keep the bulk of the mound in place.

Spirals, snaking lines and sun rays were pecked or carved into the rock by hand using stone tools. They are impossible to decipher today but when you are looking at them, you are looking into the minds of Neolithic people who conceived these designs to convey sacred messages. Climbing on top of the central mound is worth the effort for the fine views west along the River Boyne and south-east to Newgrange.

If travelling independently you can stop off at nearby Dowth to see what Newgrange and Knowth looked like before their rediscovery, excavation and reconstruction. This massive hummock in the corner of a field has a refreshing air of abandonment but is perhaps best appreciated once you have been to the rebuilt temple tombs. Nineteenth-century excavation and quarrying have left the mound looking like a crater. Once again you have a great view of Newgrange from its top.

The passage tombs of Brú na Bóinne fell out of use about 2000 BC, when their massive mounds were slipping outwards and small communities were by then living around them. They attracted myths long after the tombs' original purposes were lost to memory. In the medieval period they were believed to be the homes of the legendary Tuatha Dé Danann, the peoples of the goddess Danu.

One of the 200 or more carved kerb stones of Knowth passage tomb

Dowth, the third major passage tomb at Brú na Bóinne, shows how Newgrange and Knowth looked before reconstruction

CORONATION PLACE OF THE KINGS
HILL OF TARA, CO. MEATH

To walk on the Hill of Tara – Temair na Rí – is to travel through 5,000 years of history and enter the world of Ireland's Celtic heroes. Tara is the legendary capital of the Tuatha Dé Danann and an inauguration centre for high kings of Ireland until the sixth century AD. The hill contains a complex of mounds and ditched enclosures with a history dating back to 3000 BC and which are only recently revealing some of their secrets.

It is the shadows of the kings that are cast longest across the recent past, for this is a place that symbolises Irish independent nationality. Four hundred Irish revolutionaries died here in 1798 and 750,000 people gathered here in 1843 to protest against the Act of Union.

The hill is a brow of short-cropped emerald grass above a wide plain which stretches for miles to the north and west as far as the three hills of Loughcrew. To the east lie low hills, on one of which stands the silhouetted ruin of a fifteenth-century church tower on the site of a monastery which once housed St Columcille's shrine. It, and the church built on the side of Tara, are perfectly placed to remind adherents to the old religion about the rising power of Christianity.

Rather than taking the footpath through the churchyard, turn right inside the wall and begin at the far end of a shallow ditch. Known as the Teach Miodhchuarta – Banqueting Hall – it is more likely to be a processional way leading to the ceremonial centres on top of the hill. As yet undated, it may relate to Neolithic or late Iron Age ceremonies on Tara. At the other end of the Teach Miodhchuarta you come to Ráith na Seanadh (the Rath of the Synods), a ring fort dating from the first three centuries AD which may have enclosed a house or religious building.

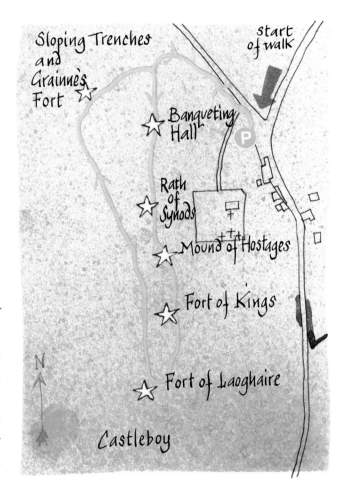

Start Hill of Tara car park
Site location N920595, OSI 1:50,000
   Discovery Map D42, Meath, Westmeath
Distance 1½ miles
Time 1 hour
Difficulty Easy
Family friendly

The ruined church tower on the Hill of Skreen is testament to the medieval spread of Christianity in Ireland which replaced the Celtic religions associated with the Hill of Tara

Next you reach the most visible and oldest monument: a 5,000-year-old chambered tomb known as Dumha na nGiall – the Mound of Hostages – after the High Kings' tradition of hosting local nobles to ensure their allegiance. A portal stone decorated with cups and rings guards the east-facing entrance to a short passage which was used for similar ancestor ceremonies to those at Newgrange. An archaeological survey in 2009 identified the postholes of a large timber circle enclosing the mound.

The mound is just inside the earthwork of an Iron Age hillfort known as Ráith na Ríg – the Fort

The first one you reach, a circular platform surrounded by three rings of banks and ditches, is known as the Forradh or Royal Seat. In its centre is a standing stone known as the Stone of Destiny. It was moved here from north of the Mound of the Hostages in 1798 to commemorate the 400 rebels who died in the Battle of Tara. If this really is the original Stone of Destiny then over 100 Celtic high kings were crowned here, and the stone is said to screech loudly when touched by the rightful king.

The circular earthwork next to the Royal Seat is known as Teach Chormaic – Cormac's House, referring to Cormac mac Airt who became a hero of medieval Irish legend as a High King of Ireland. The Fenian Cycle of myths about the warrior Finn mac Cumail are set in the reign of Cormac some time between the second and fourth centuries AD. It dates from at least 1,500 years earlier, being a prehistoric ring barrow covering a grave, a type of burial site found in many parts of Ireland which were mostly built in the Bronze Age but originated in the Neolithic and continued into the Iron Age.

Beyond this complex is another ring fort, known as Ráith Laoghaire or the Fort of Laoghaire, a fifth century king who is said to have been buried here standing upright after the forces of nature killed him for reneging on his promise never again to invade Leinster. Another legend claims he died after his Christian adversary St Patrick cursed him.

From Laoghaire's Fort walk along the slope back towards Cormac's House but keep downhill to pass the house and Mound of Hostages at a distance. If you carry straight on down the slope towards the gorse and trees you will come to a series of three circular earthworks clinging to the slope. They are known as the Sloping Trenches and Grainne's Fort. The latter is named after the daughter of Cormac who appears in a tragic love tale in the Fenian Cycle. These earthworks are actually Bronze Age ring barrows, prehistoric burial mounds which have slipped down the slope.

The monuments of Tara have a complex history beginning when the Mound of Hostages was built for Neolithic ancestral rites. At least four burial mounds were added to the hill between the Neolithic and the Iron Age, before three inter-connected ring-forts were added in the first centuries AD to crown Irish kings and become immortalised in legend as the forts of Cormac and Laoghaire.

of the Kings – which encloses the summit of Tara. The hillfort's ditch is on the inside of its bank so it is unlikely to be a defensive site. Rather, it demarcates two interlocked circular earthworks rich in Celtic mythology. They are seen as the royal centre of kingly power in Ireland between 2,000 and 1,500 years ago.

UNDERGROUND ART
LOUGHCREW, CO. MEATH

Start Loughcrew
Gardens near Oldcastle
between Kells and
Cavan

Site location N585777,
OSI 1:50,000 Discovery
Map 35, Cavan, Louth,
Meath, Monaghan

Distance 3 miles

Time 2 hours

Difficulty Moderate

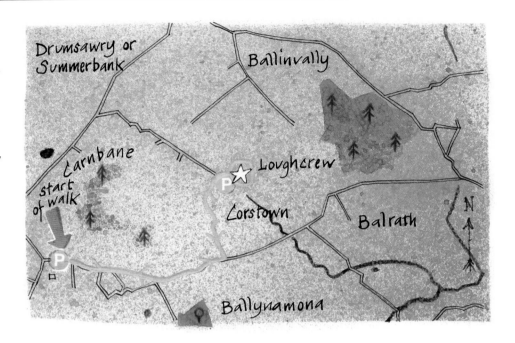

Four striking limestone hills in north-west county Meath are home to one of the largest groups of best-preserved Neolithic chambered passage tombs in Ireland. The Loughcrew hills form a craggy, grass-covered, east–west ridge which is the most prominent natural feature above gently rolling farmland which stretches as far south as the Hill of Tara.

They are also known as Slieve na Calliagh, or the Hill of the Witch, from a legend that a witch dropped the stones of the tombs as she leapt from one hill to the other. They date from the same Neolithic period as Newgrange, about 5,000 years ago, though one tomb was reused as a workshop for decorating bone pieces just over 2,300 years ago in the Iron Age.

If you visit in the summer there will be a guide to show you around and inside Cairn T. At other times of the year, call in at nearby Loughcrew Gardens for information and a key to the cairn. You can take a long or a short walk to Cairnbane East, the only hill of tombs that is open to the public. Either begin at the gardens for a round walk of about 5km (3 miles), partly along narrow country lanes, to see Slieve na

Calliagh in its setting or drive to the car park just below Cairnbane East for a walk of a little over 500 metres (¼ mile).

Whichever way you go, look out for the tombs on top of the hills as you approach the ridge. The large grey limestone mounds can be spotted among the natural crags, grass and gorse of Cairnbane West to your left and Cairnbane East to your right. The two largest tombs on Cairnbane West are deliberately positioned to be visible from either side of the ridge while the main tomb on Cairnbane East can be seen from all around. All of the tombs become hidden from view from the lower ridge.

It is difficult to say from which directions the Neolithic people approached the tombs because their settlement sites have not yet been discovered. They lived somewhere on the surrounding lower ground and walked up to the tombs from different sides of the ridge and would have seen the prominent tombs during their daily lives. It would have been important to the sense of drama during Neolithic processions on to the hills that the cairns disappeared from view as people approached.

Climb Cairnbane East from the car park following the wooden footpath posts. It is only after a steep climb and arriving on the crest of the hill that the tombs are dramatically revealed once again. The most impressive is the towering stone mound of Cairn T, surrounded by a circle of smaller satellite tombs. Once through the iron gate you will pass by the teeth-like ring of kerb stones of a cairn on your left. Like all of the other tombs at Loughcrew it is oriented on Cairn T, the ceremonial heart of Slieve na Calliagh.

The bulk of this stone focal point is secured within a ring of massive limestone slabs set on end which prevent the mass of the cairn from slipping outwards, just as at Newgrange and Knowth. Some of these kerb stones have been pushed out by the force of the mound slowly slipping outwards over the millennia. A distinctive north-east-facing block stands out from the others and may have been aligned to face the midsummer sunrise. The entrance looks out to the south-east, protected by the two largest kerb stones.

As you bend down to peer into the passage you are looking along the tunnel which people crawled into 5,000 years ago to enter the chamber at the far end. Where there is now a small grill above the chamber to give some light, Neolithic worshippers would have entered into darkness, with only the flickering smoky light from tallow candles to guide them.

Rock art is inscribed into many of the sandstone

Chambered tombs on Cairnbane West

ABOVE *Rock art carved on sandstone slabs deep in the chambers inside Cairn T*

RIGHT *Slieve na Calliagh looking at Cairnbane West from Cairnbane East*

slabs which were brought from further afield to line the passage and chamber. Two slabs just inside the entrance on the left are covered in pecked-out cups and circles, easily seen from outside. Natural light from the entrance reaches as far as a pair of upright portal stones which narrow the passage and seem to guard the dark prehistoric underworld beyond. Past the portal stones and set in opposing walls of the passage are two slabs completely covered with dozens of small cup marks that make the stones look like weather-worn bones. Once past these slabs you need to climb over a stone sill to enter the chamber itself.

This is a wondrous artificial cave, with three dark mouths leading off into side chambers to form a cross shape with the passage, like all of the other tombs in Loughcrew. With the aid of a torch, the carved and grooved art inside these side chambers jumps out from the stone slabs and then recedes again into the gloom. Surface after surface is decorated with ornate designs including concentric circles, zig-zags, curves, cups, radial disks and striated ovals. Three disks on the far wall of the end chamber, each with what look like rays emanating from their centres, may represent the passage of the sun across the sky. This wall is illuminated by the first light of sunrise during the equinoxes.

Once outside again, you will find each ruined satellite tomb is a smaller version of Cairn T. By going through the gate in the fence on the opposite side of the ridge you can walk back to the car park along the southern slope of the hill keeping a large thicket of gorse on your left. The main peak in front of you is Cairnbane West.

There are even more tombs on the western hill and while two are as big as Cairn T, they are all built to face the central tomb of Cairnbane East. Neolithic people may have processed along the whole ridge from one hilltop group of tombs to another during elaborate ceremonies. Perhaps individual communities held rites at the smaller tombs with the bones of their ancestors before gathering together for larger ceremonies culminating at Cairn T.

Keep an eye out for more recent history on the ground too. The low ridges that cover the pastures like green corduroy, grouped within long boundaries of banks and ditches, are the remains of cultivated fields that may have been abandoned as little as 150 years ago. You can follow one of the banks and ditches immediately below the western side of the summit back to the footpath to return to the car park or Loughcrew Gardens.

OVERLEAF *Sunrise from the rear of Cairn T*

BETWEEN THE LOUGHS
URAGH, CO. KERRY

Start Tousist
Site location V832635,
    OSI 1:50,000 Discovery
    Map D84, Cork, Kerry
Distance 7½ miles
Time 4 hours
Difficulty Difficult
Family friendly

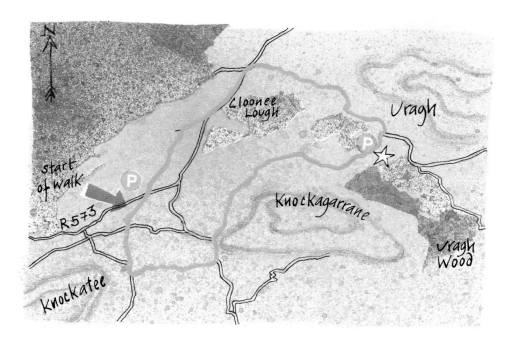

Uragh stone circle in Co. Kerry is probably set in one of the most beautiful locations of all stone circles in Britain and Ireland

Most of the spectacular stone circles set in beautiful countryside are famous and well-visited, such as Avebury, Castlerigg and Callanish. But every so often, you come across one that is hidden away, a gem that receives very few visitors yet takes the breath away when you see it. Uragh, on the Beara Peninsula in the far south-west of Ireland is just such a place.

This distinctive circle was built some time between 2500 and 1500 BC on a shoulder of land between two loughs under the shadow of mountains with cascading waterfalls. This is surely one of the most beautiful locations for a stone circle anywhere in Britain and Ireland.

You can walk to Uragh from the nearby town of Tousist by following part of the waymarked Beara Way, a long-distance footpath that circumnavigates the whole of the Beara Peninsula. The first part of the walk runs south-west from the town along narrow country lanes through small fields and scattered communities. The footpath starts at the edge of the farmland on Drumbohilly Lower and the climb up begins, passing traces of ancient boundaries,

enclosures and homesteads and on to peat bog which began forming over 2,000 years ago.

The path skirts around the northern side of the red-brown rocky peak of Knockagarrane, a sugar loaf mountain rutted and ridged from millions of years of erosion, with views right across Kenmare Bay to the mountains of the Ring of Kerry. Eventually, breathtaking views are revealed of the Cloonee Loughs, a string of lakes running from the bay into the mountains. In the morning, they shimmer like jewels among pale-green grasslands and woodlands, while just after sunrise mist clings and swirls above their surface. The loughs are fringed with craggy mountains on which you find some of the Beara's finest and most isolated walking.

The path drops down towards a ridge between Cloonee Upper Lough and Lough Inchiquin, where you can make out the small circle of five stones beside a tall blade-like outlier. The path passes a farm sheltered among trees and rough grazing for sheep, until it reaches the level boggy ground beside the water. The stone circle is now hidden beyond the ridge and it is only as you climb up on to the top that it is revealed once again.

Nothing can quite prepare you for the sight of this stone circle. Five short stones crowd around at ungainly angles beneath the 3 metre (10 ft) high outlier, which seems to direct the circle towards Lough Inchiquin like a giant weather vane or ship's rudder. The lough runs deep into the mountains and is fringed with woodlands along its southern shores. Waterfalls drop down the mountain at the far end of the lough during wet weather.

A small prehistoric farming community who lived long before the land was blanketed in peat bog built Uragh as their arena for ceremonies. There are dozens of similar stone circles in south-west Ireland, but none is so spectacular as this.

The community would have grown crops on fertile soil, raised livestock on lush grasslands and caught fish from the teaming loughs. Perhaps they built their stone circle here on this ridge to give thanks for the abundance of food on land and in water, or to play host to ceremonies relating to the water itself. Offerings made to water, either in bogs, lakes or rivers, are common throughout prehistory and the shore of Lough Inchiquin below has many flat rocky outcrops that could have served as platforms for throwing objects into the lough. It may have been towards the end, or some time after the stone circle fell out of use, that the weather worsened and a wetter, colder climate buried the fertile farmland under thick blanket peat.

After visiting the circle, return to the footpath and continue east to a minor road via the nearby car park. Follow this to the busy R571, along which you will have to walk a short distance until you can pick up a minor road back to Tousist.

Stone circles like Uragh were built when a warmer, drier Bronze Age climate allowed people to live and farm the now peat-covered uplands

OVERLEAF *The full splendour of Uragh's location is only revealed once you climb on to its ridge between Cloonee Upper Lough and Lough Inchiquin*

ROCK AND A HARD PLACE
POULNABRONE, CO. CLARE

Start Poulnabrone car
park on the R480 north
of Ballydoora Cross.
Site location M236003,
OSI 1:50,000 Discovery
Map 51, Clare, Galway.
Distance 1000 yards
Time 30 minutes
Difficulty Easy
Accessible

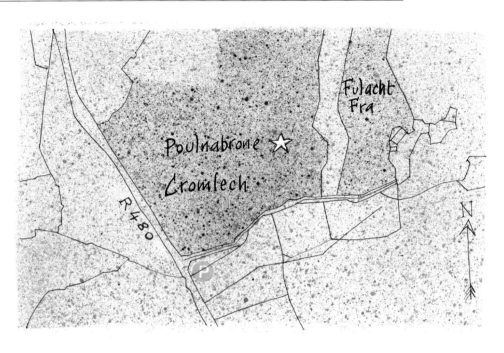

OPPOSITE *Poulnabrone stands on the
limestone pavement of the Burren, which
is sprinkled with colour during spring
and early summer*

OVERLEAF *The fallen back stone of
Poulnabrone's chamber*

The hard, grey limestone skeleton of the Burren rises up above Galway Bay and the fertile green lowlands, where lush hedges are alive with may blossom and gorse. The Burren is a vast plateau of unremitting limestone pavement: lines of grey rock divided by dark shadows of joints and fractures. When the sky is overcast, the colour is leached away, and the light is transformed into a dull monochrome which flattens the three-dimensional landscape.

Climbing on to the Burren, whether on foot or by vehicle, is to ascend to another world. However, it has not always been like this. Visiting the Poulnabrone dolmen is to look through a portal into a past over 4,500 years ago before the Burren was transformed into this stark, alien landscape.

Ordinarily a stone tomb such as Poulnabrone dolmen would stand out against a grass field, but not on the Burren. On first sight the stone slabs of the dolmen are lost among the fractured blocks of grey limestone pavement around it. Sadly, Poulnabrone does not lie on one of the Burren's footpaths so the only way to visit it is by driving or cycling along the road from Ballyvaghan to Corofin.

The approach from the nearby car park is heavily landscaped and the dolmen is hidden behind grey limestone walls. Tour groups buzz around it, coming and going for 30-minute halts on whistle-stop coach tours of the Burren. A site that could so easily disappoint requires a little time, plenty of imagination and ideally a visit late in the day to watch the sun go down and witness a little bit of magic as colour is brought back into this grey world of stone.

Avoid the temptation to walk straight over to the dolmen, and instead carry on over the limestone pavement beyond the tomb to approach the dolmen from the front and to get a feel for how the characteristic Burren landscape is today.

The land dips gently down towards the south from low cliffs and a narrow gorge created by a spring in the north-east. North to south aligned fissures split the limestone into round-edged longitudinal blocks which are eroded by water into patterns of dimples and hollows. The fissures hold water in this barren land so are flush with green and, during late spring to early summer, patches of colour as orchids, guelder

would have been visible from the outside. Stone-robbing for walls has exposed the chamber, just as the rocky skeleton of the Burren has been revealed by erosion following the loss of the prehistoric forests.

The magic of light happens at Poulnabrone when the setting sun is close to the horizon. Its rays reach into the exposed chamber so that the underneath of the capstone glows for a short while with a warm orange light. You will only see the cold grey limestone being dispelled on a sunny evening by being close to the dolmen, an illumination missed by those tour parties who stop to tick-off Poulnabrone.

Poulnabrone was excavated in 1985, when a cracked portal stone that now lies beside the tomb was replaced. The bones of approximately sixteen to twenty-two adults, six children and a newborn baby were found inside the chamber. Only the larger bones were found and these were not laid out as individual burials.

The people interred in Poulnabrone were defleshed elsewhere after they died, then some of their larger bones were taken to be placed together in the tomb alongside carefully chosen objects such as a polished stone axe, flint and chert tools, fragments of pottery, two stone disc beads, a perforated bone pendant, a bone pin and two quartz crystals.

The community who lived and farmed in the area around the tomb probably made the deposits over years as parts of ancestor rituals. They couldn't know that over the generations, their descendants would slowly strip away the soil and woodland, eventually making it all but impossible to live and farm on most of the Burren. Pockets of soil survived for smaller populations to farm during the Iron Age over 2,000 years after Poulnabrone was built. The homes of these Iron Age communities, dating from the first thousand years AD, survive as ring forts dotted across the plateau. Caherconnell Fort lies 1,000 yards to the south of Poulnabrone.

If you wish to walk across the Burren to discover other dolmens and ring forts you can find walking routes in local tourist information points. They are all reminders of a more fertile past when the bones of the Burren were fleshed out with soil, fields and trees.

roses, primroses, dwarf gorse and vetches come into flower.

Look carefully to find low banks of stone criss-crossing the ground. These may be ancient field boundaries, hinting at a past when the land was very different. During the Neolithic period, when Poulnabrone was built, the Burren was a fertile plateau dominated by pine forests. Elms and hazels grew alongside the pines while the woodland was broken in places with open grasslands where the dolmen builders pastured cattle and grew crops. They built at least seventy dolmens during the centuries around 2500 BC across this productive land to mark their territorial claims.

Poulnabrone is the most impressive dolmen to survive, and as you turn back towards it you can make out its graceful form. A thin limestone capstone, almost rectangular, rests at an angle on top of four narrow limestone uprights, each almost 2 metres (6½ ft) high, which define two sides of a tomb. You are approaching the original entrance and the nearest uprights are the portal stones guarding this entrance. As you get nearer you can make out the entrance's sill stone slotted into one of the natural east–west aligned grikes.

The dolmen is built on top of a low stone and earth mound. When it was built and used about 4,500 years ago the dolmen was a chamber buried deep in a stone mound. Only the entrance and possibly the capstone

TOMBS WITH A VIEW
CARROWKEEL, CO. SLIGO

Though Carrowkeel is on top of the Bricklieve Mountains it is overshadowed by Carrowmore, its better-known cousin down on the plain to the north-west. Both are cemeteries of Neolithic chambered tombs, similar in date and form to Loughcrew.

Carrowmore is the largest Neolithic cemetery in Ireland, and its setting on rolling farmland beside a road makes it one of the top prehistoric destinations for tourists to Ireland. Visiting Carrowmore is a highly managed experience, similar to going to Stonehenge. Carrowkeel on the other hand has a wilder feel and offers views of at least five Irish counties as well as Donegal Bay.

Today you can walk to Carrowkeel and back from Castlebaldwin, following part of the Miner's Way waymarked long-distance footpath as far as the car park for the monuments. The route brings you to the dramatic Bricklieve Mountains – long fingers of dark peat-covered limestone separated by green, cliff-edged gorges – which rise out of the surrounding farmland of green fields and hedges.

From a distance you can make out the grey mounds of the Neolithic chambered tombs on top of the ridges. There are more than twenty in total and they were deliberately placed on such prominent locations about 3000 BC or earlier to be seen by people living in and moving about the lowlands. They are made from grey limestone blocks quarried from the mountains, which heightens their visual impact. As you get closer to the Bricklieves you are rewarded with views of the dramatic limestone gorges which run south into the mountains and carve the Bricklieves into beautiful ridges, each seemingly topped with another prehistoric mound.

The narrow road along a gorge turns into a rough track as it climbs on to the ridge where three tombs with public access are found. For the final approach you walk across blanket peat, which formed thousands

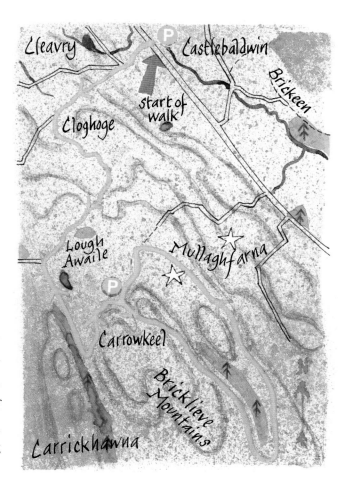

Start Castlebaldwin
Site location G755115, OSI 1:50,000
Discovery Map D25, Sligo (E), Leitrim, Roscommon
Distance 7½ miles
Time 4 hours
Difficulty Difficult

LEFT *Mullaghfarna plateau on the eastern side of the Bricklieve Mountains once was home to the Neolithic community who built the Carrowkeel tombs*

BELOW *One of the limestone gorges of the Bricklieve Mountains*

The three Carrowkeel chambered tombs with public access

of years after the tombs were built, to reach each of the tombs in turn on successively higher ground. The top of the ridge presents views of the Sligo countryside, an undulating patchwork of hedgerows and pastures which runs for miles until it reaches the mountains on the northern and eastern skylines. Lough Arrow shimmers in morning sunlight as it meanders below the length of the Bricklieves to the east.

Each mound appears to be a fairly untidy 3 metre (10 ft) high dump of limestone blocks without any architectural form or design. On closer inspection each has an entrance buried in its north-west side, which faces the distinctive hump of Knocknarea Mountain outlined in front of the sea 24 km (15 miles) away. Even at this distance it is easy to see its summit crowned by a massive Neolithic burial cairn 10 metres (33 ft) high and 55 metres (180 ft) in diameter. Knocknarea dominates the plain of the Carrowmore Neolithic cemetery, and was obviously an important regional ceremonial centre for the different Neolithic communities living around it.

The entrance of the first mound is framed by three horizontal limestone slabs, and you have to bend, twist and turn to squeeze between the sill and lintel to enter the dark chamber. Moist warm air envelopes you with an earthy pungency. Entering the chamber was made

difficult to heighten the importance of the ceremonies and of the people who were privileged to have the right to enter inside this underground otherworld to commune with the gods and conduct ancestor rituals with bones from recently dead individuals.

The chamber's corbelled roof is supported on three pairs of upright stones, each of which mark the entrance to a side chamber. Where the decorated sandstone used to line the chambers at Loughcrew gives a warmth to those interiors, the unadorned limestone of Carrowkeel looks stark and cold.

You can spot many more cairns from the three mounds on this ridge, and if you are here early in the morning or late evening, they all glow like orange beacons in the sunlight. When the tombs were built during the Neolithic, the Bricklieves were grassy hills rising above the wooded and boggy land below. Some communities may have lived in clearings on higher, drier ground connected to each other by forest paths, as well as on foothills and lower mountains, such as on Mullaghfarna plateau here on the Bricklieves.

To find the plateau, turn right when you are back on the rough track and walk around end of the ridge towards Lough Arrow for a fantastic view across a gorge of limestone cliffs to a narrow flat-topped plateau edged with more cliffs. A chambered tomb

ABOVE *Inside one of Carrowkeel's limestone chambers where the bones of ancestors were kept*

stands out on its highest point, while the flat ground of the plateau is covered with over 150 small ruined stone round houses closely packed together. It is difficult to make them out from this distance and the only public access is along a very faint path to the south of the tombs.

Imagine this area with smoke rising from the thatched roofs of these densely set round houses and people milling around, working in fields or herding sheep and cattle. These may have been the people who built the Carrowkeel chambered tombs, and recent excavations dated three houses to between 3000 and 1500 BC, broadly contemporary and later than the tombs.

You can walk on to Mullaghfarna plateau by heading south along a very indistinct footpath above the cliff to the east of the cemetery, before dropping down into the hidden valley then skirting around the peak to come on to the plateau. From the north end of Mullaghfarna plateau you can drop down into the dry valley and head north to pick up the rough track back up to the tombs and return to Castlebaldwin.

Most of the path from the tombs to Mullaghfarna isn't at all clear, so it's only advisable if you're confident about safely navigating across open moorland and around cliffs with a good map and compass.

OVERLEAF *Carrowkeel Neolithic chambered tombs and views north across County Sligo*

DRAGON'S TEETH
BEAGHMORE, CO. TYRONE

Start Beaghmore car
park on a road north of
Dunnamore
Site location H685843,
OSNI 1:50,000 Discoverer
13, The Sperrins
Distance 1,000 yards
Time 30 minutes
Difficulty Easy
Accessible

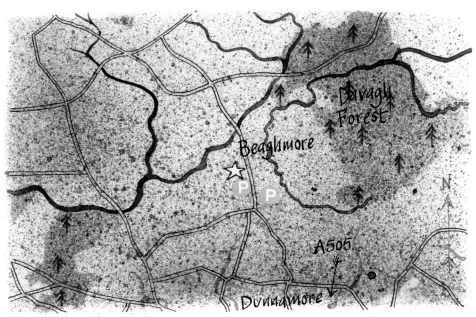

Beaghmore is a place designed to encourage a belief in fairies or leprechauns. This complicated arrangement of interconnected stone circles, rows and cairns was only discovered in the 1940s when farmers found the mostly shin-high stones while cutting this part of the Sperrin Mountains for peat.

Though the Sperrins have many walking trails, the only walking in this area is along narrow country lanes with many blind bends and summits. Beaghmore is therefore a site to arrive at and explore at leisure. By doing so you can wander along the routes created by the stone rows when they were built over 3,000 years ago in the Bronze Age.

It is little surprise that these stones stayed hidden under peat for so long. They are not as tall as the stones of Callanish, which remained above the peat bog on Lewis. At Beaghmore, most of the stones are only between 10 and 20 cm (4 and 8 in) high with a few 'giants' 1 metre (3¼ ft) tall. Luckily the peat cutters told the authorities before any damage was done and the site was excavated later in the 1940s then again in the 1960s. The site is now displayed and protected under grass and it is likely that even more prehistoric

features remain buried under the peat on the gently sloping hillside nearby.

If the size of Beaghmore seems underwhelming, the complexity of the arrangement of the circles, rows and cairns is bewildering. It takes a little time to walk around the site to get an idea of how they all fall into place. There are seven stone circles, six of which are placed in pairs with a cairn between them, ranging from 10 to 20 metres (33 to 66 ft) in diameter.

The one circle which stands alone is possibly unique in Ireland in being filled with over 800 small upright stones known locally as the 'Dragon's Teeth'. Ten stone rows lead tangentially towards the edges of the circles; sometimes towards the cairns in the gaps between the paired circles. The rows radiate out from the group of circles towards the north-east and usually comprise one long row of short stones next to a short row of tall stones. There are twelve cairns around the edges of the circles and most of these cover a cremation burial.

The prehistoric builders of Beaghmore were clearly taking a lot of care in choosing, placing and arranging the stones without the desire to create a grand monumental statement in stone like at Stonehenge, Avebury or Orkney. This must have been an important place for communities to gather and hold ceremonies throughout the year. There are many other small circles and stone rows in the region so it is likely that each individual community living in this area had its own ceremonial centre which it used over generations.

In some ways Beaghmore is more akin to the Hill O'Many Stanes in Caithness, and may have been a place for observing the rising or setting of the sun and moon, though there are no accurate alignments. They may also have been a local community's response to deteriorating soil fertility and encroaching peat brought on by a worsening climate or over-use of the land. Excavations found Neolithic fields below the stones but the relationship between the date of the circles and the date of the peat is unclear.

The peat formed over the foothills of the Sperrin Mountains later in prehistory to create today's open upland landscape, possibly beginning to spread on to land used for farming some time between the Bronze and Iron Ages from 4,000 to 2,000 years ago.

The views from Beaghmore take in this vast expanse of rolling blanket bog with the higher range of the Sperrins to the north-west. Beaghmore is on a small outlier of the mountains, a mostly level plateau rising to the peak of Slieve Gallion to the east. This would have been prime land to cultivate and live on during the Neolithic and, at least, the early Bronze Age.

Today's better farmland is in the wide, gentle valleys around Cookstown, Dunnamore and Draperstown, but these would have been damper and more difficult to farm in prehistory. If Beaghmore is a community's response to changing climate it is a testament to a world turned upside down, when families tried to halt the inevitable transformations and eventually had to abandon the higher ground.

A stone row bisects one pair of stone circles at the complicated arrangement of Bronze Age ceremonial structures on Beaghmore

One of Beaghmore's pair of stone circles looking towards the Sperrin Mountains

BURNING RING OF FIRE
NAVAN, CO. ARMAGH

Start Navan Fort car
park on the road
from Tamlaght
Site location H847452,
OSNI 1:50,000
Discoverer 19,
Armagh
Distance 1 mile
Time 30 minutes
Difficulty Easy
Family friendly

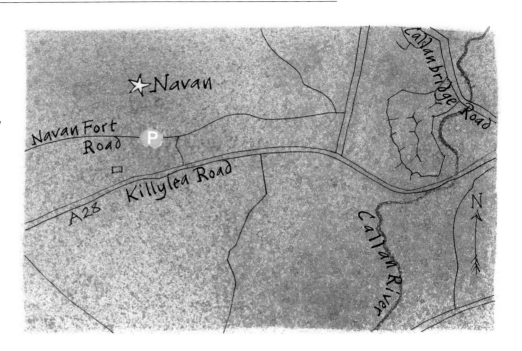

Navan is one of the most intriguing structures surviving from the Iron Age. It is often referred to as a fort and the medieval storytellers who told the cycle of legends called *The Táin* in the eighth century AD or earlier claimed it was Emain Macha, the capital of the Kings of Ulster. The stories of *The Táin* are wonderfully interpreted at the nearby Emain Macha Navan Centre, which also explains how the finds from the archaeological dig identified a much stranger story buried below the grass-turved mound.

The steep yet short walk from the roadside is much like taking a stroll in a wooded hillside park. Soon you come across the first remains from the past: a high bank and deep ditch, to the sides of which bluebells cling in spring. At first sight, the bank and ditch look defensive – the ground of the hill has been steeply cut back and would be difficult to climb without today's concrete steps.

But wait. The ditch is on the *inside* of the bank, contradicting defensive wisdom which would want to force attackers to try and cross the ditch under assault from defenders on a rampart above. Perhaps the Ulster kings of *The Táin*, laid low and unable to fight

by a curse, had no need for defences as they waited for Connacht's Queen Medb to attack and claim the fertile bull Finnbhennach she desired.

It is best to keep walking and thinking. As you steadily climb the hill, an artificial mound enclosed within a bank comes into view on top. It is easy to imagine a large wooden hall on top of the mound protected within a strong palisade fence running around its circumference. This must be the main hall of the Kings of Ulster, possibly even the fort of the legendary King Connor. Yet it's strange that there are no obvious entrances through the boundary, or that the top is not flat enough for a large building fit for a king.

Views from the top take in a landscape of hedges, pasture fields and trees rolling off into the distance. To the east, Armagh's two churches dedicated to St Patrick dominate the skyline. St Patrick made Armagh the centre of the Irish church so that the Christian religion had its base close to Emain Macha.

Archaeologists have indeed found a massive wooden circular building on top of the hill. At over 40 metres (130 ft) in diameter it required 280 large

oak posts arranged in five rings to support what must have been an extraordinarily heavy roof. Radial lines of these posts divided the building into thirty-four sections – significantly, the same number as the tribes mentioned in *The Táin*. The wall was made from planks and an entrance in the west led to four parallel rows of posts which created three aisles ending in the centre. Here was the largest post of all, a huge tree trunk standing at the very centre of the building. The tree rings of this post show that it was felled around 95 BC.

This is by far the largest building ever found from Iron Age Europe. You would expect such a building to be the hall of a powerful king, a legendary king whose life would be later recalled in myths such as those found in *The Táin*. But the building was never lived in. It was filled with a massive stone mound rivalling Newgrange in size. Thousands of limestone boulders were piled up inside the building to create a flat-topped cairn almost 3 metres (10 ft) high. The building's plank wall kept the cairn from tumbling outwards.

Then the strangest event of all occurred. Brush-wood was piled up against the wall and deliberately set alight. The building burned. Where you stand now on this quiet grassy knoll was turned one day in 95 BC into what may have been one of the biggest bonfires ever seen in the Iron Age. The flames would have raged for days, lighting the night sky for miles around and filling the air with a towering column of smoke.

After the smoke cleared and the ashes cooled, the unburnt parts of the building were removed, and the cairn was carefully covered in layers of turf and soil until it was buried 2.5 metres (8 ft) below the surface of the mound. This was the last archaeological evidence for activity on top of Navan, suggesting the firestarters walked away, never to return.

Clearly a lot of people were involved in constructing the wooden building and the cairn. The ditch and bank around the hill were probably created at the same time to contain the event. The building's thirty-four sections may represent thirty-four communities or clans who gathered together to conduct this amazing incident. The big question is: why on earth did they do it? Why go to all that trouble to build such a fantastic structure, only to then burn it down?

This was a ceremony on the grandest of scales, a transformative act that altered a large number of people's relationship with something through the use of fire. Was that something each other, the gods or the earth? Perhaps there were parallels with Caesar's accounts of Gauls burning sacrificial slaves in large wicker men to communicate with the gods. There are Scottish Iron Age hillforts which were so comprehensively burnt with such a heat that their rocks vitrified, causing some archaeologists to suggest this could only be the result of deliberate fires rather than warfare. Archaeologists are also beginning to discover evidence for similar burnt structures to Navan elsewhere in Ireland.

Perhaps at Navan a representation of the cosmos or of the communities of the region was built and burnt as an offering to the gods. Whatever happened here in 95 BC was of such a magnitude that the folk memory of the event burned brightly, and many, many generations later the writers of *The Táin* associated the hill with the capital of Ulster and the home of King Connor.

ABOVE LEFT *The turfed mound of Navan buried a surprising secret*

ABOVE RIGHT *The ditch and bank that encircle Navan hill*

SCOTLAND

CEREMONIAL GLEN
KILMARTIN GLEN, ARGYLL

Nether Largie Stones at Kilmartin with the central stone decorated with up to twenty-three cup marks

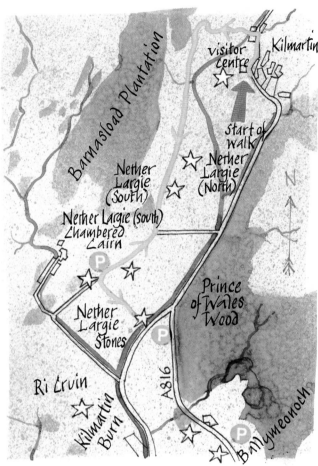

Start Kilmartin village

Site location NR828979, OS 1:25,000
    Explorer map 358, Lochgilphead &
    Knapdale North

Distance 4–6 miles

Time 2–3 hours

Difficulty Easy
Accessible

The flat valley floor of Kilmartin Glen is home to one of the largest surviving prehistoric ritual centres in Scotland, on a par with the better-known sites at Orkney and Callanish.

Here a ceremonial and cemetery complex of stone circles and tombs was first laid out about 5,000 years ago in a line running for over a mile alongside the burn. The sites were modified and built upon for over 1,000 years until the centre ultimately comprised seven large round mounds of stone, two stone circles and a stone

row with a cup-marked stone. Another two tombs, parallel stone rows and a henge are located just to the south of the linear cemetery.

Over 150 archaeological sites survive in the glen and on the low hills, including rock art, burial chambers, standing stones, crannogs, hillforts and brochs. Most are on private land and only the heart of this complex at the bottom of the glen is accessible to visitors.

The best place to begin is at the Kilmartin House Museum in the village, found perched on a narrow shoulder of flat land on the eastern side of the glen, which is set among the dramatic scenery between Oban and Lochgilphead. The museum has a great exhibition on the prehistoric monuments of the glen and an atmospheric audio-visual show.

Squat houses form a ribbon of white-washed walls stretching either side of a solid-looking brown

church. Before you set off on the walk you can look in the churchyard to see medieval carved grave slabs decorated with knot designs and spear-carrying warriors. Continue north through the village and take the lane on your left to drop down on the valley floor to begin your encounter with the ancient linear cemetery.

The glen is a flat band of pasture ringed by low ridges of craggy hills where woodlands mingle with sheep-grazed grassland, giving the impression that this was where 'Capability' Brown must have found inspiration for his eighteenth-century 'picturesque' style of landscaped parks. The slowly meandering burn is all that remains of a wide, fast-flowing river that scoured the glen after the end of the last Ice Age, approximately 10,000 years ago. If you visit in early summer you may be rewarded by the sight of hares surging between lines of freshly mown hay. A nineteenth-century coach

Nether Largie South Cairn was built by prehistoric farmers in a fertile glen still important for agriculture

Temple Wood is a stone circle embedded in a low cairn of pebbles with a stone grave cist in its centre

road, now partly a tree-lined path and partly a quiet lane, runs parallel to the linear cemetery and gives access to the different monuments.

The first and largest chambered tomb of the cemetery is the Glebe, just below Kilmartin village which stands at 4 metres (13 ft) high and over 33 metres (108 ft) in diameter. Like the other four mounds of the linear cemetery, the Glebe covers a complex series of ceremonial sites that were used for hundreds of years before the cemetery was completed. Under the Glebe lies a double ring of stones, within which two stone boxes, known as cists, contained burials with grave goods.

You can see under the next cairn, Nether Largie North, where the original stone cist is displayed inside a modern chamber along with a carved stone decorated with cup marks and the outlines of axe heads. The third cairn was partly robbed for road stone in the nineteenth century along with two others that no longer exist except as cropmarks. Standing on

top of this mound gives a good impression of the scale of the cemetery, with views along the valley bottom to the other cairns to north and south. The massive mounds are all built from grey water-worn pebbles gathered from the glen, so they stand out against the green background of the fields.

Walking south along the coach road you'll pass rough heather-clad ground, which rises abruptly from the valley floor where cattle graze in the summer. The glen then widens out to form a natural amphitheatre, forming the home for the most complicated section of the cemetery.

You'll come first to Nether Largie South Cairn, a chambered tomb that was originally a trapezoidal cairn, later enlarged into a round mound. The north-east-facing entrance of the earlier tomb has been exposed and actually sits above the remaining pebbles of the later mound. Two vertical slabs frame a narrow entrance that leads down in to a 6 metre (20 ft) long stone chamber divided into four compartments.

You can still enter the chamber which had a floor covered with burnt human bones among which was placed a pot that dates to 2500 BC. About 500 years later, three pots known as beakers were placed on top of some of the earlier bones and the entrance was blocked with a stone slab. This was about the same time or just before all the large mounds of the cemetery were built above the earlier burial cists and ceremonial monuments. This transformation of the ritual landscape was made at roughly the same time as metalworking was introduced into Britain.

From Nether Largie South Cairn you now have a view south where the glen widens into an expanse of flat fields used for hay and pasture. The five yellow-brown standing stones of Nether Largie Stones spring up from the ground to your left, while two circles of short, tooth-like stones are shaded within the grove of pines and oaks of Temple Wood to your right. To get an idea of what the original ceremonial sites looked like before the mounds were built, continue along the lane to Temple Wood. The pair of stone circles dates to 3000 BC, the same date as the features which lie underneath the mounds. The low cairns of rounded pebbles that fill and surround the circles were added over a period of 1,500 years, along with cremations buried in the shallow stone boxes.

From Temple Wood a short walk takes you across fields to Nether Largie Stones, passing a solitary standing stone which leans towards the row as if desperate to join in. The row is also aligned along the glen and would have been a short route for processions between Nether Largie South Cairn and the southernmost mound. Two pairs of tall standing stones mark the start and end of the row, the focus of which is a distinctive scimitar-like standing stone nearly 3 metres (10 ft) high, covered in cup marks on its southern side. A small stone circle would have been the focus of ceremonies held here.

Return to Kilmartin by retracing your route. If you wish to visit Ballymeanoch stone rows, mounds and henge a little over 2 km (1¼ mile) to the south of Nether Largie Stones, it is safer to return to Kilmartin first and drive to Dunchraigaig car park rather than walk along the busy A road. Two parallel lines of standing stones, one with four stones, the other with two, are the survivors of a 4,000-year-old avenue running north to south along the glen in a similar setting to Nether Largie Stones. Two of the stones are decorated with cup marks. The avenue may have been part of the ritual

A rainbow arcs above Nether Largie Stones during a brief interlude in a torrential summer rainstorm

complex to the north or a separate ceremonial centre altogether.

You can create longer all-day walks by heading north out of the village to first visit the Kilmartin Eye about a mile away. This is an art installation of five decorated timber posts which evokes the sense of enclosure, common to the prehistoric monuments of the glen. About 6 miles beyond this is Ormaig rock art, found within a forestry plantation on the top of the ridge north-west of the village. You can return to the village via Camasserie Castle.

Ballymeanoch Stone Row is part of a Neolithic avenue in Kilmartin Glen

ROCK ART
ACHNABRECK, ARGYLL

Start Achnabreck car
park

Site location
NR855906,
OS 1:25,000
Explorer map 358,
Lochgilphead &
Knapdale North

Distance 1,300 yards

Time 30 minutes

Difficulty Easy
Family friendly

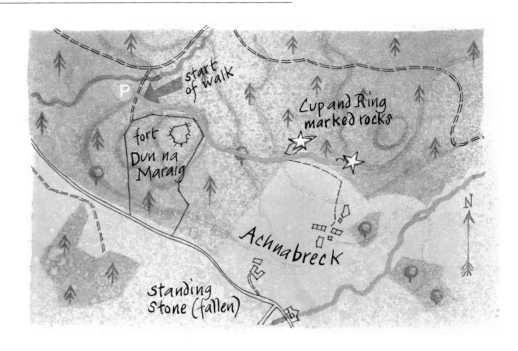

While you are at Kilmartin it is worth visiting Achnabreck a little to the south. Here, lost in a vast Forestry Commission plantation, are huge, publicly accessible areas of prehistoric rock art. While nearly all of Kilmartin's rock art is on private land, the inscribed outcrops of Achnabreck are easily visited along a signposted trail from a car park. They are great places for families to ask their children what they think the designs represent and why prehistoric people might have carved them where they did.

There are four areas of rock art along a path which leads up a gentle slope from the left of the car park. A short walk takes you through the ranks of conifers, partly screened with birch, rowan and alder. After a short while you come across a domed surface of dark red rock covered in cup and ring carvings that together form the most extensive area of prehistoric rock art in Britain. There is a fourth decorated surface further along the path.

There are rows of small cups and concentric rings that enclose cups, sometimes with a line running through all of the rings from the centre

Britain's most extensive area of prehistoric cup and ring carvings are at Achnabreck in Argyll

outwards. They were probably made about 5,000 years ago during the Neolithic period, though it is almost impossible to date art carved into natural rock unless the stone has also been used to make a structure such as a chambered tomb with dateable archaeological evidence.

The rock, though surrounded by the plantation, is still a prominent landmark on a low-lying ridge above a glen. In prehistory, the conifer-cloaked valleys and hills were a much more open mix of woodlands, grasslands and fields.

Nearly all of the outcrops in Argyll chosen by prehistoric people to carve their designs are found at places where you gain a change of view as you walk. Some archaeologists suggest that the rock art was made on routes and that it was a way of communicating to travellers that they were entering the lands of different communities. The act of carving would have been very important, possibly accompanied with storytelling and rituals that re-affirmed the communities' use of their land. Or they may have been part of sanctifying natural places which were turned into ceremonial sites because of the nature of their landform.

The beauty of abstract rock art is that we will never be sure what the designs mean and why the locations were chosen, so anyone can speculate about the intentions of those who made it.

The route takes you past Dun na Maraig, a hillfort on top of a densely forested rocky knoll which uses the hill's cliffs for part of its defences. Little is known about this unexcavated fort, though it is probably one of the early settlements of the Dál Riata Scots who lived in Ireland and Argyll.

THE TWIN TOWERS
GLENELG BROCHS, HIGHLAND

Start Glenelg

Site location
NG829172 OS
1:25,000 Explorer
map 413, Knoydart,
Loch Hourn & Loch
Duich

Distance 5½ miles

Time 3 hours

Difficulty Moderate
Family friendly

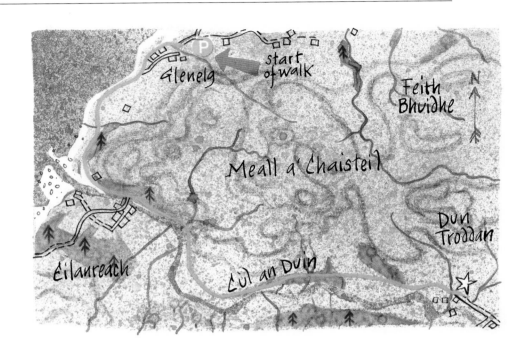

The walk from Glenelg into the narrow Glen Beag will take you from a quiet village with a golden beach deep into a forested Highland glen of towering crags. The destination is an encounter with mainland Scotland's two most impressive Iron Age brochs, before returning along the same route to Glenelg and a view over the Sound of Sleat to Skye.

From Glenelg, follow a narrow lane along the lower slope of the south-facing mountainside a little above the river. It snakes through thick scrub and woodland of birch, alder and copper beech, among other native deciduous species. After a while this gives way to narrow pastures bordered by bramble-entwined dry-stone walls of the local dark sandstone. There are small crofts here and there, and sturdy cattle graze the riverside fields.

The southern side of the glen is overshadowed by the 740 metre (2,430 ft) summit of Beinn a' Chapuill, its imposing heights crowned by grey shards of Lewisian gneiss, which splinter through the green grass and shine black in the sun when wet after rain.

The road rises and falls gently, following the contours of the mountainside, as it picks out the best route

RIGHT Dun Telve is one of a pair of Iron Age brochs in Glen Beag near Glenelg

OPPOSITE The imposing dark red tower of Dun Telve

between the steeper slopes above and the floodplain below. This is most likely the line of the Iron Age route into Glen Beag, which probably passed through much the same landscape of deciduous woodland on the lower slopes, open valley sides above and rough grazing on the glen floor. The valley sides may have been more wooded and Iron Age farmers may have grown oats or barley in small valley floor plots. The one major new development is the conifer plantation, which takes up most of the southern side of the glen.

One more bend and suddenly the dark red-brown circular tower of Dun Telve is above you, the gradual narrowing of its circumference emphasising its height

which survives at its original 12 metres (39 ft). You can still enter through the same north-west-facing door that its Iron Age inhabitants used over 2,000 years ago.

Like all brochs, Dun Telve is a dry-stone, double-skinned wall bound together with stone lintels and an internal stairway which wound up inside the wall to an upper floor. The builders used a detailed knowledge of force and stress to construct these double walls, which were much higher than timber or single stone walls would allow. There are approximately 700 brochs in Scotland, found from the west to northern coast, the Western Isles and Northern Isles, built between 600 BC and AD 100.

The ground floor was for storage and livestock, while the family lived on the upper floor, the timbers of which were supported on stone escarpments protruding from the inner edge of the wall 2 metres (6½ ft) above ground level. You can still climb part way to the upper floor up the surviving stairway. Escarpments at the very top of the wall held the beams that supported a conical roof. If you visit in the evening you are likely to see and hear red deer; they often come down to the broch when the glen falls into shade during dusk. The Iron Age families of Glen Beag would have hunted deer like these.

Continue along the road and look for the rising land on your left for the second broch. Dun Trodden is built on a knoll within a cleft in the mountainside above valley floor 500 metres (¼ mile) from Dun Telve. It is built in almost exactly the same way and also has a north-west-facing door. Slightly less of Dun Trodden survives, but again you can see the escarpments and follow in the steps of its Iron Age inhabitants up the internal stairway. There is a great view along Glen Beag down to Dun Telve, which looks majestic as it rises above the trees.

These brochs are much closer to each other than the Orkney brochs of Eynhallow Sound. Are they the only two to survive from a densely settled Iron Age glen, or are they the sign of two important families who needed to live close together, either for security or to keep an eye on each other? It is also possible that they date from slightly different periods, one family moving from one to the other if the earlier one partly collapsed.

Brochs were once thought to be defensive, similar to medieval fortified manor houses, and while deterrence probably was important, they are now understood to have been built to impress on others the status of the families who lived in them. Perhaps the proximity of the Glenelg brochs to each other is a case of Iron Age one-upmanship.

GNEISS WORK
CALLANISH, LEWIS

Start Lay-by for Callanish 3 on the A858

Site location NB213330, OS 1:25,000 Explorer map 459, Central Lewis & Stornoway

Distance 3½ miles

Time 2 hours

Difficulty Moderate Family friendly

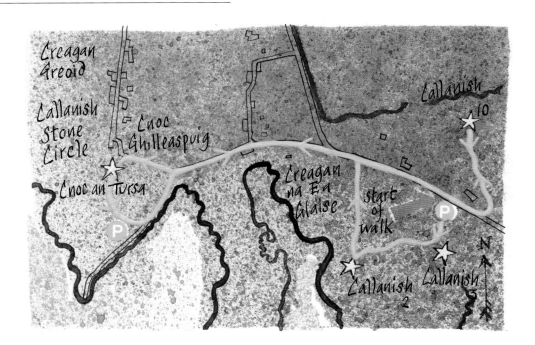

Callanish, or Calanais in Gaelic, is one of the most astounding stone circles in Britain and Ireland – partly for its situation as guardian of the sea lochs below, and partly for the grandeur of the tall twisted and textured gneiss stones, carefully height-graded towards the pinnacle, with its central monolith.

Callanish was built during the Neolithic, some time between 2900 and 2600 BC, replacing a century-or-so-old history of arable farming on the ridge with a major ceremonial monument which formed the centre of a constellation of at least eleven stone circles by the shores of Lochs Ròg and Ceann Hulabhig. This Neolithic ritual landscape rivals, in its scale and design, contemporary sites on Orkney and the later monuments at Avebury and Stonehenge.

A half-day's walking will take you comfortably to four of the circles – and afford you stunning views over heather moors and lochs towards distant mountains. Perhaps you will also be lucky enough

The impressive stone circle and a spectacular location make Callanish one of Britain's most spell-binding prehistoric monuments

to see golden eagles soaring in the sky or seals and otters swimming in the lochs.

To appreciate the landscape setting of Callanish as well as the other circles, it is really best to begin a little way down the road at Callanish 3, known in Gaelic as Cnoc Fhillibhir Bheag. We cannot be sure whether different circles were visited in succession by large groups processing from one ceremony to another, or whether the smaller circles were used by families who then gathered together for larger rituals at Callanish.

What is clear is that the location of each smaller circle was carefully chosen to give views of the main circle with arrangements of stones or specific stones laid out in relation to the main site. This walk therefore cannot be claimed to lead you along routes used by Neolithic people, but will give an idea of how one circle would be seen from another during ceremonies.

Callanish 3 is a double circle with eight surviving stones in the outer ring and four in the inner ring. The stones of all the circles are the same Lewisian gneiss, the oldest known rock in Britain, laid down about 3,000 million years ago. It is a twisted and folded grey rock, weathered into wildly textured shapes and patterns which contain large orange and white crystals of hornblende. Two of the inner stones are clearly positioned so that the hornblende reflects the rising and setting sun. Like many of the other circles, Callanish 3 is built on a low ridge above the loch, but has its main view of the water blocked by a knoll.

Cnoc Fhillibhir Bheag – Callanish 3 – is one of at least eleven small stone circles built as satellites around the majestic main circle at Callanish

Dropping down from the ridge and crossing a low peat bog of sphagnum moss brings you to Callanish 2, Cnoc Ceann a'Ghàrraidh, which is an oval ring of five stones up to 3.5 metres (11 ft) tall. From here you can see how impressive Callanish is when it is outlined on the skyline and you can get a good idea of how the builders arranged its stones to appear to rise in height towards the centre of the circle.

Today's landscape is very different to the one the Neolithic communities knew when they built the stone circles. Loch Ròg was then a salmon-rich river coursing through fertile farmland, where the locals grew an early form of barley and reared cattle and sheep. The sea had not yet risen to today's levels, while the peat would not begin to blanket the land for another couple of thousand years. Woodlands and scrub of birch and hazel grew in the more sheltered areas; rough grazing occupied the higher land. Settlements would have been dotted across the landscape, possibly as scattered individual farmsteads or small villages similar to those on Orkney, though none has yet been discovered.

From Callanish 2, walk to the road, which will bring you to Callanish and the visitor centre. If you want to approach Callanish as Neolithic worshippers approached it, by walking along its avenue, don't head straight for the visitor centre but turn right up a steep lane and enter the monument at its northern end.

Two rows of stones converge on the central circle, which is flanked on either side by two more stone rows, and stands on a stage whose backdrop is the craggy knoll

Looking down the Callanish avenue
towards the circle and Cnoc an Tursa

The Lewisian gneiss used to build Callanish is full of texture and character, giving each standing stone its own personality.

of Cnoc an Tursa at the end of the ridge. The avenue is aligned on the centre of the almost-level ridge and to walk along it is to see the stone circle as the Neolithic communities would have done thousands of years ago. Watch how the stones and their arrangements appear constantly to shift as you get closer; some stones become hidden, others are revealed, many subtly change shape. The twisted patterns in the tall and graceful yet fantastical and magical stones give each monolith an individual personality and, depending on the natural light, the textures create intricate shadows along their surfaces while the beds of hornblende shine with specks of light.

The avenue ends at the circle which is 12 metres (39 ft) in diameter around the tallest stone in the centre which stands 5 metres (16 ft) high. A fourth stone row runs away from the side of the circle opposite the avenue towards Cnoc an Tursa.

Groups of Neolithic people probably converged on the northern end of the avenue from the surrounding countryside, then processed along it to participate in ceremonies led by religious leaders standing inside or in front of the circle itself. Some may already have attended smaller ceremonies in the nearby

circles; some may have camped in the ground below Callanish if they came from further afield. Would the ceremonies be solemn or festive? We can't be sure, but evidence from elsewhere, such as at Durrington Walls and Stonehenge, indicates that feasting was a big part of major communal gatherings. There is some thought that people gathering at Callanish may have also observed the lunar standstill, a phenomenon occurring every 18.6 years, which we'll explore further at Loanhead of Daviot (pages 174–7).

There is a chambered tomb at the base of the central monolith, added shortly after the circle was built, seeming like something of an afterthought in the way it is squashed in between this monolith and the circle. The tomb was used for several centuries before it was ransacked some time between 2000 and 1750 BC and some of its contents cast aside as debris beside it.

By 1000 BC Callanish was abandoned, its lure as an arena for ceremonies having abated after almost 2,000 years. This may have been about the time the sea levels rose and a wetter climate hastened the spread of the peat that would eventually bury the stones up to half their height. Callanish wasn't totally lost to the peat, as legends were told to explain the strange sentinels of the hill, one saying that they were giants gathered in an assembly when they were turned to stone by St Kieran. You can truly understand why medieval Christians would think these gnarled and misshapen stones huddled around a tall pillar were petrified creatures, rather than quarried stones erected thousands of years previously to facilitate a very different kind of religion.

If, after you have returned to Callanish 3, you would like to walk further, go to Callanish 10 – Na Dromannan – via a gate beyond the last house on the opposite side of the road from Callanish 3 car park.

Walk for just over 1 kilometre (½ mile) along the broad ridge where there are gneiss outcrops among the peat. Head towards a low hill topped by a cairn and you will find Callanish 10 on a prominent boulder outcrop a little before this hill. Callanish 10 has eleven large stones which were originally thought to have been freshly quarried from the surrounding bedrock but never transported to complete a circle elsewhere. Since excavation, it seems more likely to be a fallen circle that was built near a potential prehistoric quarry.

The stone which stood nearest to Callanish has a large crystal of hornblende embedded in the side that faced the main circle, and this would have glinted in the sun when seen from the main circle. The steep rock face below and parts of the bedrock on the hill may have been busy with Neolithic quarrying, as tall stones destined for the stone circles were split from the living rock by skilled craftspeople using wooden wedges and water. Fairly small numbers of people could have moved the stones on wooden rollers down the slope towards the places where they built the circles and so completed the transformation of the stones from natural rock to ritual centres.

Today's peat bogs make these direct routes down the ridge difficult to walk along, never mind move heavy stones, so the easiest way to return to Callanish 3 is back along the ridge.

Callanish's assembly of giants

BROCH ON A ROCK
DUN CARLOWAY, LEWIS

Start Dun Carloway car park

Site location NB189412, OS 1:25,000 Explorer map 459, Central Lewis & Stornoway

Distance 2 miles

Time 1 hour

Difficulty Moderate

Dun Carloway broch perches on top of an outcrop near the western coast of the Isle of Lewis

Dun Carloway has one of the most spectacular locations of all the Iron Age brochs in Scotland. The half-tumbled circular tower is perched on a rocky bastion clinging to the rugged hillside of Beinn an Dùin.

An Iron Age community chose to raise the stone tower of their round house just over 2,000 years ago in this apparently barren and bleak landscape where the rain can sheet in from the ocean at a moment's notice, and thin soils have to be dug into mounds to gain any depth for crops.

A solid curving wall, 9 metres (30 ft) tall and built above a steep cliff of solid bedrock, is silhouetted against the sky as you climb up towards it. The profile is one of an immense tooth, a shape created by much of the remaining wall having been taken down some time after the 1500s to build blackhouses in the small village below.

The path takes you around to the north-facing entrance, which you can still enter, following the original inhabitants when they built it around 100 BC. The broch is built to the same design as the Glenelg brochs; a double-skinned dry-stone wall held together

ABOVE *Dun Carloway is one of the best-preserved brochs in Scotland.*

LEFT *The interior wall of Dun Carloway stands 9 metres (30 ft) tall with a ledge running 2 metres (6½ ft) above the ground which supported the upper floor*

Dun Carloway's double-skinned dry-stone wall is a masterpiece of Iron Age architectural engineering

with slab-like stone lintels and an internal stairway which winds up inside the wall from the ground to the first floor. The stairway was accessed from the low door in the wall opposite and the timbers of the upper floor were supported on the ledge built into the wall about 2 metres (6½ ft) above the ground. The ground was used for livestock and storage while the family lived on the floor above, with either one more floor above them or a high roof used for more storage and for preserving food by smoking it above the fire.

The views from Dun Carloway are breathtaking, with Loch an Dùin forming a triangular bowl of water below and the Atlantic Ocean extending as far as the eye can see beyond the jagged coastline. The sea views of many brochs led early antiquarians to mistakenly think that the island brochs were signal towers built to warn of Viking invasions during the ninth century AD.

The surrounding area is open peat grassland, broken here and there by lines of grey Lewisian gneiss, and looks to all intents and purposes like an upland landscape, despite it being just above sea level. Ruined blackhouses and modern bungalows alternate with each other along the single-track road above the loch, their long, thin walled fields running ruler-straight down to the water's edge.

If you want to get a good idea of how Dun Carloway looks in the landscape, carry on past the broch and on to the top of Beinn an Dùin to see how the tower balances on its outcrop with the loch far below. A circuit around the peninsula north-west of Dun Carloway allows a short exploration of this typical landscape on Lewis's western seaboard. Short stone-capped peaks jab out of peat-filled hollows, brown heath intermingles with bright green grass, and the sea gashes its way into the land in a series of small bays and inlets. There is no escape from the elements

The view from Dun Carloway across the peaks of Suil Bhiorach towards the Atlantic Ocean

here, and the weather tends to blow in rough from the Atlantic, filling the air with a salty keenness which rasps at your face. Hills form one darkening ridge after another to the south.

As you turn south past Rinavat and then east to pick up the end of Dun Carloway's single-track road, you find a great view of the village laid out below its broch, which reinforces your sense of the lengths its builders went to find a prominent and secure platform for their home. Whether they chose the location for defence or show, or some of both, they chose extremely well.

A NEOLITHIC POWERHOUSE
MAES HOWE, RING OF BRODGAR AND STONES OF STENNESS, ORKNEY

Start Stones of
Stenness car park 5
miles north-east of
Stromness on the
B9055

Site location
HY306126, OS
1:25,000 Explorer
map 463, Orkney –
West Mainland

Distance 4 miles

Time 2 hours

Difficulty Easy
Accessible

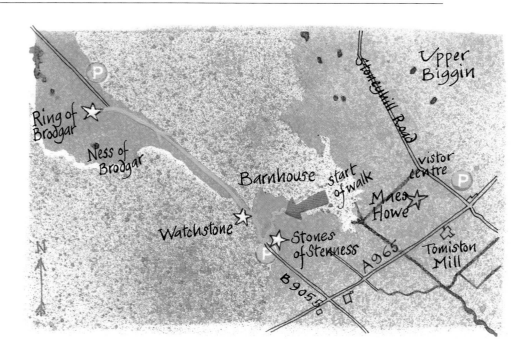

Orkney has some of the best-preserved and most impressive prehistoric monuments in Britain, each of which is highly photogenic with a fascinating history and situated in an amazing landscape.

Many of the best-known Neolithic sites are listed as the Heart of Neolithic Orkney World Heritage Site, and are found on Mainland by the shores of Lochs Harray and Stenness. Within in this arena are a series of massive ceremonial monuments and two settlements, which date from 5,100 to 3,500 years ago. These are Maes Howe chambered tomb, the Ring of Brodgar, the Stones of Stenness, the Watchstone, and the villages of Barnhouse and Ness of Brodgar. By themselves, any of these monuments would make the trip to Orkney worthwhile.

You can still walk between the monuments along the processional route which Neolithic people may have used, as well as entering them through their

original entrances. Only Maes Howe is difficult to reach on foot due to a busy road, but hopefully that will be addressed if plans for a new visitor centre go ahead.

To appreciate the Neolithic landscape, we will begin at Barnhouse, a lochside settlement on the northern side of the Stenness peninsula, where you can wander in and out of the doors of four reconstructed buildings. Barnhouse was only discovered in 1984 when archaeologists identified the foundations of fourteen stone houses occupied between 5,100 and 4,800 years ago. Each house was a squat oval building between 5 and 7 metres (16–23 ft) in diameter with thick sandstone walls supporting a conical turf roof. Inside were two rectangular rooms each with a central hearth and small chambers built into the walls. The largest house may have been a communal building.

There are views to all the other ceremonial

OPPOSITE *Sunset over the Watchstone from the Stones of Stenness*

The large house at Barnhouse, possibly a communal building or 'temple'

The Watchstone is one of a pair which guarded the avenue between the Stones of Stenness and the Ring of Brodgar

monuments, including the Ring of Brodgar, elevated on a dark slope of land above the shimmering loch. Where today there is tranquillity and carefully mown grass, in Neolithic times the settlement would have been full of activity as people prepared animal skins, made clay pots and disposed of their rubbish. Thick middens of hearth ashes, animal bones and broken pots built up over time. The insides of the houses would have been dark, lit only by natural light from the door, the light of the hearths, and candles or oil lamps.

A route led from the village to the Stones of Stenness, a stone circle and henge contemporary with Barnhouse which stands just 200 metres (650 ft) away. The only entrance to the stone circle is aligned on Barnhouse, so by approaching the stones from the village you are following in the footsteps of Neolithic families attending ceremonies. Four of the eleven original thin

flagstone stones still stand, the tallest towering above you at 6 metres (20 ft) high. Neolithic ceremonies were likely to have been lively, noisy affairs with music, feasting and dramatic rituals centred around a hearth that cast dancing shadows from flickering firelight.

You can see both Maes Howe and the Ring of Brodgar from the circle. From Stenness it is a short distance to the slender Watchstone, the survivor of a pair of tall stones that framed the tip of the peninsula at the start of an avenue along the Ness of Brodgar to the Ring of Brodgar. You can follow the approximate route of this avenue along the road and a causeway across the lochs. Was there a Neolithic causeway too? Look out for the remaining stones of the avenue in the gardens of houses to your left and, after the second house, the location of another village contemporary with Barnhouse.

As you continue along the avenue, rising land hides the Ring of Brodgar so that when you get close it makes a dramatic appearance of standing stones silhouetted

against the sky. A short uphill walk on to a low ridge brings you to this massive henge and stone circle via a solitary standing stone which is the only survivor of three or more.

At over 130 metres (426 ft) in diameter, the Ring of Brodgar is one of the largest henges ever built. Thirty-six of the original sixty stones survive, each an angular flagstone block standing up to 4.5 metres (15 ft) high, forming a ring of jagged teeth on the skyline. They are all the more striking as the sun sets behind them. The Neolithic builders built the henge on ground that slopes down to the east to welcome the midsummer sunrise or moonrise, while also creating a dramatic frame for the midwinter sunset and moonset. The Ring was built during the early Bronze Age about 500 years or so after the Stones of Stenness and Maes Howe, either to replace Stenness or to expand the ritual landscape.

The view back along the route you have walked shows the Stones of Stenness with Maes Howe in the distance. Maes Howe seems to lurk in the landscape compared to the stone circles which declare their presence with more authority. Access is much more restricted than at the stone circles, and the mound's actual arena for rituals is hidden deep inside compared to the stone circles' prominent presence in the landscape. It is a distinctive turfed mound which protects one of Northern Europe's most impressively engineered chambered tombs under a cap of clay, earth and stone. It easily compares with Egyptian tombs in terms of its scale, standard of construction and massive size of stones.

The entrance is along a straight passage flanked by long flat-sided slabs, the same size as those that stand upright at the Stones of Stenness. Inside is a large square chamber with walls of yellow and orange sandstone blocks, which originally converged about 6 metres (20 ft) above head height to a corbelled roof. Ancestral bones would have been deposited inside three raised chambers in the walls during elaborate rites. As at Newgrange, the entrance to Maes Howe is aligned so perfectly on the sun that at one time of the year this chamber fills with golden light. But where the passage at the Boyne celebrates midwinter sunrise, Maes Howe is turned south-west towards midwinter sunset.

The sheer scale of Maes Howe poses the question: was this the very heart of ceremonies for the Neolithic communities of Brodgar, Stenness and further afield? Its scale, standard of construction and massive size suggests a monument used by more than a single small community, possibly drawing in people from a large area, to celebrate the most important day of the annual cycle and the bones of people's ancestors.

VILLAGE OF THE SANDS
SKARA BRAE, ORKNEY

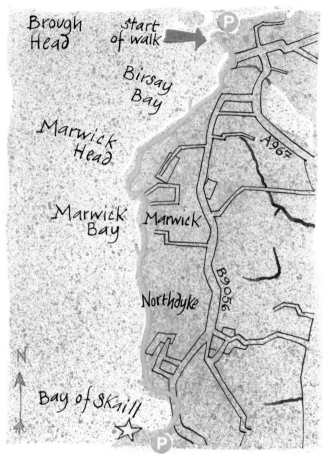

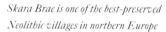
Skara Brae is one of the best-preserved Neolithic villages in northern Europe

Skara Brae lay buried beneath the dunes of the Bay of Skaill on the western coast of Orkney Mainland for thousands of years until a wild storm in the winter of 1850 stripped away its covering of grass and sand. The storm revealed northern Europe's best-preserved Neolithic village, a tightly packed cluster of small stone houses which were the homes to families about 5,000 years ago.

You can visit Skara Brae from the visitor centre or make it the destination of a coastal walk beginning and ending in Birsay, 10 km (6 miles) to the north, which takes you along the rugged coastline where steep sea cliffs afford plenty of opportunities to spot seabirds, seals and occasionally whales.

The route is a trail through time, beginning opposite a Viking village on the Brough of Birsay, which you can get to along a narrow causeway at low

Start Birsay
Site location HY232188, OS 1:25,000 Explorer map 463, Orkney – West Mainland
Distance 12 miles
Time 6 hours
Difficulty Moderate
Accessible

tide. The walk then passes the Knowe of Buckquoy, a grassy oval mound over stone walling which may be an ancient settlement, then the sixteenth-century Earl's Palace, which was the home of Robert Stewart, an illegitimate son of King James V of Scotland, then the memorial to Lord Kitchener south of Marwick Head. Around Marwick Bay you pass the Knowe of Flaws, one of numerous burnt mounds found near the coast, an undated settlement recently excavated before it eroded into the sea, and an early chapel.

At the northern end of the Bay of Skail is the Iron Age broch at the Knowe of Verron, where you can see a sandstone floor, hearth and the bases of internal walls. A little further on at Snusgar archaeologists have excavated a three-room, split-level Norse house which has one striking similarity with Skara Brae – the inhabitants abandoned it as it was covered in sand.

From here you can see orange and yellow sandstone slabs piled above the beach. These are identical to the ones used by the Neolithic families of Skara Brae to build and furnish their homes.

The landscape you have walked through has changed a little in the 5,000 years since people lived at Skara Brae. Today large pastures run inland from the coast to the peat-cloaked hills, with virtually no trees in sight. There was a sparse covering of birch, hazel and willow scrub during the Neolithic period, probably growing in small patches divided by large grassland pastures with small arable fields clustered around other villages. As you walk along Skaill Bay you have to imagine the coastline extending much further out to sea where it ended in cliffs, and the area of the bay as flat land containing a small loch. Driftwood from the virgin forests of North America was regularly washed up on shore.

The flagstones eroding out of the Bay of Skaill were put to good use to make walls and other domestic structures by the Neolithic people of Skara Brae

One of Skara Brae's narrow underground passages leading to the Neolithic houses

Inside one of Skara Brae's Neolithic houses, with its stone 'furniture' built around a central hearth

When you see the mounds of Skara Brae at the south end of the bay, imagine a village in Neolithic times as a huddle of turf and stone mounds, part buried into the ground near to the loch, with small fields sown with barley during summer and larger areas of open grassland grazed by cattle and sheep.

People seem to appear and disappear into the ground beside the roofs. They are entering a low, narrow stone-lined subterranean passage where they crouch and squeeze their way below a slab roof to reach side passages that take them to the doors of their houses. The only light is what might leak in from the far ends, natural light from outside and orange firelight from the hearths. The doors are low to keep out the Orcadian winds, and people have to crawl through them to enter their houses where they can at last stand up inside their smoky homes lit by the flames of the fire burning in the central hearth.

Visiting Skara Brae is well managed and you look down into stone-lined passages, nine houses and a workshop from a path skirting the tops of the walls. It is a view of the village as if the original conical turf roofs were picked up and put to one side.

Each house was a single square room with stone walls and fitted with built-in stone furniture which appears to comprise a dresser opposite the door and a pair of box beds to either side. The dresser was used either to store household goods or to display prized possessions. Small stone boxes set into the floor may have been used to store pots or for food preparation. Small alcoves are built into the walls of each house; some are easy to reach while others are hidden behind the dressers.

The central fire provided light and warmth, probably along with oil lamps burning fat from marine mammals and sea birds, while the roof offered a little ventilation. Archaeologists have found flint and bone tools, fragments of clay pots, bone jewellery and haematite polishers inside the houses.

Three things are most striking about Neolithic life in Skara Brae. The families lived cheek-by-jowl with each other yet had total privacy behind doors barred with wooden poles or whalebones. They laid out their homes in exactly the same way, suggesting a strong degree of conformity between the families. None of the houses is grander than

Looking through a Neolithic door. This is the low doorway into one of the houses at Skara Brae

the others, which makes it unlikely that there was a single chief or ruling family.

The Neolithic people of Skara Brae formed a close-knit community that thrived for generation after generation over a period of 500 years. Then the sands began to move in, and the underground homes were so buried that the families were eventually forced to move and find a new place for their village.

SOUND OF THE IRON AGE
BROCH OF GURNESS, ORKNEY

Start Evie Bay car park
Site location HY383268
   OS 1:25,000 Explorer
   map 463, Orkney –
   West Mainland
Distance 3 miles
Time 2 hours
Difficulty Moderate
Accessible

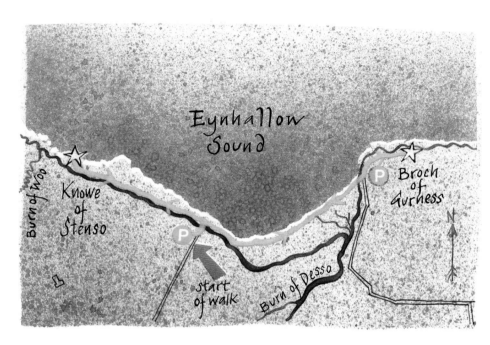

A walk to the Broch of Gurness is a coastal stroll through a gentle grassland landscape peppered with Iron Age brochs. The shores of the Orkney Mainland and Rousay either side of Eynhallow Sound contain at least eleven of these towers. While most are uninvestigated ruins, grassed-over mounds of tumbled stone, two excavated sites give a clear insight into Iron Age Orcadian life around 2,000 years ago.

Begin at the western end of Evie Bay, a sandy beach backed with sea-tumbled yellow and orange pebbles, which ends to the east at the rocky Point of Hellia, upon which the Broch of Gurness was built over 2,200 years ago. The mainland rises from verdant pastures beside the coast, past the collection of cottages that makes up Evie village, to form a horizon of dark moors where deep peat is still cut for cottage fires. The waters of Eynhallow Sound are turbulent and treacherous, as currents from the Atlantic and North Sea are funnelled towards each other with the ebb and flow of the tides.

OPPOSITE ABOVE The Broch of Gurness looking over Eynhallow Sound towards Rousay

OPPOSITE BELOW The Bay of Evie with the Broch of Gurness silhouetted against a shimmering Eynhallow Sound. Iron Age brochs line both sides of the sound

Beyond the Sound lies Rousay, a small ridge of rock with gentle slopes above the sea, which can glow bright green or glower dark brown depending on the light. This is a moody landscape where land and sea meet in patterns of light and shadow, and where the water connects as much as it separates. The sea's role as a communication channel is presumably one reason that so many brochs were built along its shores.

Instead of making straight for the Broch of Gurness, first walk along the sand and pebble shore in the opposite direction to the ruined Knowe of Stenso Broch to see how these sites tend to look before they are excavated. Ruined stone walls peek out from the grass of the prominent knoll, which is slowly being eaten away by stormy seas.

You can see six other brochs from here, although most are so ruined that you'll need good eyesight and a map to identify them all. They are distributed at regular intervals along either shore at the Point of Hisber, Knowe of Grugar and Aikerness on the mainland, and at the Knowe of Burrian and Westside on Rousay. Still visible from a distance are the Broch of Gurness and Westside's Midhowe, the middle broch of three.

In the Iron Age all the brochs would have stood out as imposing yellow-orange towers against a backdrop of land and sea. Such prominence was one of the reasons that important families built brochs – each creating a local show of strength and prestige in a battle of one-upmanship. Once one family had built a broch others would have followed suit. The families cultivated small crop fields around the brochs and their villages, while further away lay open grazing land looking much the same as it does today.

Retrace your route from the Knowe of Senso then walk along Evie Bay, either along the beach or the

entrance, which leads straight through an apparent jumble of stones to the broch's door. The broch is a double-skinned circular stone tower which survives to 8 metres (26 ft) high but was originally much taller and covered with a tall thatched roof. As you approach the broch you will get a clearer idea of the ruins that encircle the tower, discerning doors among the jumble of walls, which lead off from either side of the entrance into the small dwellings of the forty-or-so families who belonged to this community.

These days the low ruins of walls, hearths, furniture and pits are preserved in a well-kept lawn, but if you take yourself back to the Iron Age you will find yourself enclosed within a cramped passage between stone walls and thatched conical roofs. The views of the broch, Eynhallow Sound and Rousay are lost behind these roofs which cluster around the tower. Smells of cooking, fires, straw and sweat assail you from any open door you pass, as do the sounds of people talking, working and arguing. Perhaps a couple of children dart from a door and push past you to run down the passage, their mother shouting after them.

Ahead of you is the wooden broch door, below the thick sandstone lintel, either wedged shut against the wind or open as the family return from working in the fields or visiting a neighbouring broch. Stooping slightly to pass through the door, you enter a narrower passage with low doors on either side leading into small rooms built inside the broch walls.

The inside of the broch is much grander than the houses you have passed, with stone beds, a well and a hearth dominating the ground floor, and a wooden ceiling above. A flight of stone steps leads up on your right to the second floor, where there may have been another hearth to smoke fish hanging high up above your head from the rafters of the tall roof.

You can still climb these stairs, though today they give you an expansive view of the surrounding land and sea, as well as a clear look at the outline of the surrounding houses. You can wander in and out of the houses, walk through the original doorways and stand beside the hearths where families squatted to cook and get warm.

Afterwards you can return along your outward route to your starting point. Look out for seals, which are regularly seen in the Sound, and basking sharks, much rarer visitors.

track above, until you come to the Broch of Gurness. The broch was discovered as recently as 1929, when Orcadian Robert Rendall was sitting on a stool atop a mound on Aikerness to sketch the great view of Eynhallow. The leg of his stool suddenly gave way as it plunged into a hole and, on digging around the hole, Rendall found a staircase in the broch tower. Over the coming years the complicated settlement that you can see today was excavated.

To get the best impression of how the site developed and was lived in, begin by walking around the triple concentric rings of ramparts and ditches, now partly lost to the sea. These were built first, before construction began on the broch, between 200 and 100 BC as the home for the head family of this Iron Age community.

When you reach the far side of the broch, you are standing at the remains of an impressive walled

THE LONG TOMB
GREY CAIRNS OF CAMSTER, CAITHNESS

The Hill O'Many Stanes is an aptly named multiple row of small standing stones dating from the Bronze Age

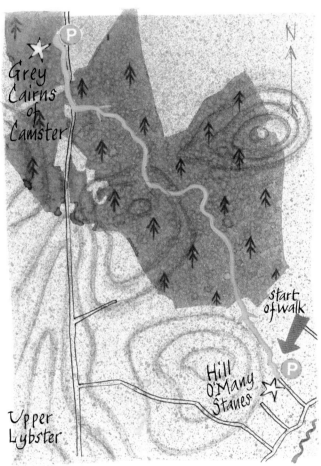

One of the most awe-inspiring prehistoric monuments in Scotland is tucked away in Caithness on high upland peat bog a few miles from the North Sea coast. Transport them to Wiltshire and they would be one of the more famous monuments in Britain.

'Grey Cairns' describes well how these massive chambered cairns look, but doesn't come close to suggesting their visual impact. Three round cairns were built here about 5,000 years ago during the Neolithic period, but the descendants of the builders had grander ideas for two of the cairns which they joined and extended into one of Britain's most striking prehistoric monuments.

You can easily visit the Grey Cairns from the adjacent car park, reaching them elevated above the bog on discrete boardwalks. But to get a real idea of how this part of north-east Scotland has changed since prehistory it is best to take the 19 km (12 mile) walk along a forestry track from the Hill O'Many Stanes.

Start Hill O'Many Stanes
Site location ND26014420, OS 1:25,000
   Explorer map 450, Wick & The Flow Country
Distance 12 miles
Time 5 hours
Difficulty Moderate
Accessible

The Hill O'Many Stanes is the intriguing site of the largest multiple stone row in the region and dates to about 4,000 years ago, or the early Bronze Age. On first appearance it looks more like an Antony Gormley art installation, with over 200 shin-high stones protruding from the heather in at least twenty-two rows, which fan out from north to south. There may have originally been about 600 stones, making it a large structure despite the diminutive size of the individual stones. It is thought the rows were some form of astronomical observatory. You may therefore be standing where Bronze Age people looked along the lines of stones to watch the moon or stars on the horizon.

From the Hill O'Many Stanes, follow the line of the single track road north-west towards the conifer plantation and continue along the rough forestry track. At the other side of the plantation join the Lybster road which takes you to the Grey Cairns. The land around the Grey Cairns is the vast undulating peat bog of Camster Moor, dominated by sphagnum moss, heather and cotton grass. Large tracts have been planted with regimented rows of dark green conifers, and these border the cairns to east and west. Soon after leaving the plantation you catch your first sight of the cairns sitting on a ridge between the plateau and a small valley, the grey weathered surfaces of their rocks contrasting with the darker earthy colours of the moors and forests.

Neolithic farmers originally built three large round cairns on what was probably the edge of good farming land, where they grew crops and raised livestock at a time when the climate was warmer and drier than today. The builders chose the ridge because it made the cairns visible for miles from a southerly arc from east to west. Sadly the conifer plantation means you are relatively close to the cairns before you see them today.

Each cairn has a south-east-facing passage that leads into a central chamber inside the mound. A later generation decided these cairns were not enough and incorporated two of them into one long monumental cairn over 60 metres (200 ft) long and 2 metres (6½ ft) high with a forecourt at either end. This long cairn is the most visually striking as it drapes itself along a sloping ridge, growing higher towards its upslope end where it rises over the two original cairns to create a heaving profile. It looks like a giant beast at rest.

You approach the cairns from the south-east, walking towards the entrances of the passages and experiencing the dramatic grandeur of the long cairn. This is probably the same direction that the Neolithic people would have walked towards them. Today you walk along a boardwalk raised above the peat bog which has developed since the Neolithic period. The cairn builders were able to walk on solid earth.

The Grey Cairns of Camster are some of the best preserved and most striking Neolithic chambered tombs in Britain

For the most striking view go to the round cairn first, which places the long cairn behind and in a slightly elevated position. It is built from small blocks of angled sandstone, which were originally contained within a low supporting wall which now only survives to either side of the passage.

You can enter the passage, if you're able – for the passages here are the narrowest and shortest of any in this book. You have to either crawl on hands and knees or squat down on your haunches and slide one foot in front of the other to move forward. There is just enough light from the entrance and a skylight in the chamber to see your way so you get an idea as to how the passages would have been experienced by the Neolithic people who came to conduct ancestral rites. Every so often a sharp corner jabs towards you

The entrance to Camster's round cairn with the long cairn in the distance

from the stone wall, but there is room to pass.

The passage feels like it will go on for ever before you can eventually straighten and stand upright in the chamber deep inside the heart of the stone mound. It is a small corbelled dome divided into two areas by tall uprights, two of them forming portal stones at the entrance of the chamber. Neolithic people left behind burnt human bone, flint tools and pottery from the rituals they carried out here. The last prehistoric generation to use the chamber blocked it behind them, leaving two human burials in a sitting position among the blocking stones. Were they guardians of the chamber, or people from one important family who claimed antecedence over the others?

Once you have squeezed yourself back along the passage and outside, continue along the boardwalk up

to the long cairn, where you will arrive at the highest and widest end. The two passages look out like tiny eyes in the side of the behemoth. Before you enter either passage, take time to go to the very end of the cairn, which ends in a high vertical wall above a low stepped platform, itself ending as two curving horns protruding outwards from either side.

This forecourt was a focal point for ceremonies where groups of people gathered to face religious leaders standing on the platform. Perhaps it was only the religious leaders who entered the chambers to conduct the rites with the ancestral bones, or maybe other people entered in ones or twos with bones of their own families. The two passages are similar narrow, low squeezes to that of the round cairn, though one is much shorter.

Retrace your route to the Hill O'Many Stanes. The communities who built the Grey Cairns over 5,000 years ago and Hill O'Many Stanes 1,000 years later lived on fertile land. Then a colder and wetter climate developed during the Iron Age, causing erosion and mineral loss from soils no longer protected by trees.

Over many generations, the descendants of the builders of the Grey Cairns and Hill O'Many Stanes found it increasingly difficult to survive, as the soils lost their fertility and the peat spread. Two Iron Age brochs show that it was still possible to live here but the population was probably much smaller by then. The good soils eventually became the peat bogs which dominate today's landscape, along with the conifer plantations for which the Forestry Commission thought this land was best suited.

Neolithic people squeezed along this narrow passage into the chamber of Camster's round cairn to hold ancestor ceremonies with little or no light to show them the way

SUNSET OF THE DEAD
BALNAURAN OF CLAVA, INVERNESS

Balnauran of Clava is a cemetery of Bronze Age chambered tombs arranged along the flat gravel terrace of Strathnairn, a few miles to the east of Inverness. They have given their name – Clava – to a type of prehistoric ceremonial funerary cairn surrounded by a stone circle found only in northern Inverness-shire. This makes Clava the best place to explore these unique prehistoric tombs and circles.

You can use Balnauran of Clava as the start of an 8 km (5 mile) walk along quiet country lanes to explore the valley landscape of the cairns, or just visit the cairns themselves, which are easily accessible on flat ground from the adjacent car park. At least seven cairns survive and more have probably been lost in the 4,000 years since they were built.

Four are accessible, three seeming to shelter like ghostly sentinels in an area of woodland next to the car park, and the fourth half a mile further along the lane. Together they form a Bronze Age cemetery built around 2000 BC, then re-used and expanded in about 1000 BC.

There is a sense of majestic tranquillity as soon as you enter the woodland where the row of three large grey cairns within their encircling stone circles loiter below the thick canopy of oaks and birches. Each cairn is over 15 metres (50 ft) in diameter and survives to over 2 metres (6½ ft) high.

They are built from grey river-worn cobbles, some of which were taken from the houses of an older settlement demolished to make way for the cairns, and they are contained within a base of kerb stones graded to increase in height and darken in colour towards the south-west. The significance of this direction is matched by the stone circles, which also become higher towards the south-west. The red sandstone circle of the eastern cairn has a towering

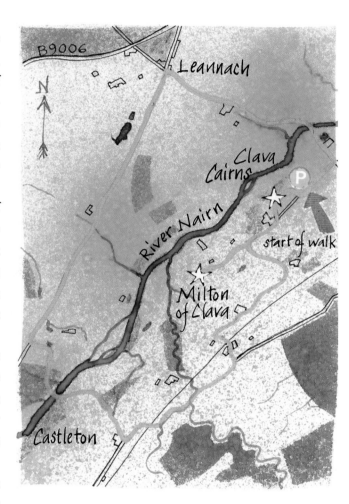

Start Balnauran of Clava car park
Site location NH7572044438, OS 1:25,000
  Explorer map 422, Nairn & Cawdor
Distance 5 miles
Time 2 hours
Difficulty Moderate
Accessible

ABOVE *The impressive bulk of Clava's western cairn imparts permanence to the Bronze Age burial site*

LEFT *The burial chamber and passage of Clava's eastern cairn*

thin slab at its south-westernmost side. Look out also for cup and ring rock art in boulders incorporated into the eastern cairn's kerb and the chamber of the western cairn.

The eastern and western cairns contain walled burial chambers that were originally roofed and could be entered by crawling along narrow, low passages, also facing south-west. The central cairn has no passage and probably never had a roof, encouraging comparison with some stone circles in Aberdeenshire which marked the locations of funerary pyres.

So why is such significance given to the south-west by the Bronze Age builders? Each cairn and circle faces the winter solstice sunset for ceremonies when the sun set before the longest night and its last rays shone into the chambers along the passages. Then the communities who built the cairns knew the dark winter nights would get no longer and they could look forward to the rebirth of the year, heralding another spring with newborn calves and lambs alongside the next sowing season for their crops. Perhaps the dead buried inside the cairns were worshipped as the people who could ensure that the gods brought the spring back again.

After visiting the third cairn, leave the woodland by the gate and walk along the lane towards Milton of Clava. The valley is a broad, flat expanse of fertile soils and river cobbles running north to the Moray Firth, the sides rising gently in a series of natural terraces, where bands of gorse and broom form yellow ribbons across the pastures. Conifer plantations create dark green borders to the east and south while the main railway line from Inverness to Pitlochry is carried across the valley by a sturdy yet graceful Victorian viaduct. If you visit between spring and summer you'll almost certainly hear and see black and white oystercatchers fluttering over the fields.

Only the south-westerly stone of the Milton of Clava cairn still stands sentinel. A rectangular ruin of stone walls beyond the cairn is all that remains of a medieval chapel, where a single stone stands

proud of the walls as if aping the prehistoric standing stone. This appears to be an attempt by the early Christian church to take over an ancient ceremonial site that may still have attracted legends, if not some worshippers, at the time. Christians in the Middle Ages often built churches near ancient sites to show the dominance of the new religion.

After visiting Milton, return to the lane and turn right up the slope on to the top of the valley side. By following the lanes you can take a circular walk that leads you under then over the railway line, down into the valley to cross the River Nairn and then on to the other side of the valley. The road verges are crammed with yellow-flowering gorse and broom, alongside the delicate creams and pinks of dog roses as well as plenty of brambles.

To the north-west there are views to Culloden Moor, scene of the last fateful battle of the Jacobite rebellion in 1746, while the dark mass of Beinn Bhuidhe Mhór lurks to the east. At the crossroads sign posted to Culloden, turn right and drop back down into the valley to return to the car park. There is a fine view of the viaduct before you rejoin the lane to the car park at Balnauran of Clava.

As you walk, strip away the conifer plantations, electricity pylons, modern farmhouses and the large pastures to imagine the valley as it would have looked 4,000 years ago. Small areas of mixed conifer and broadleaf woodlands replace the regimented stands of the huge plantations, broken here and there by

clearings where farmers tended small fields of pasture and crops. Their homes were timber round houses with thatched roofs, either dotted individually along the valley or clustered in small groups. Much of the valley floor would have been cleared to provide grazing for cattle and sheep, which would have also created the clear lines of sight needed to view the midwinter sunset from those evocative cairns.

Balnauran of Clava, better known as the Clava Cairns, is an atmospheric alignment of Bronze Age burial cairns and stone circles set in a wooded grove

MARKING OUT THE MOON
LOANHEAD OF DAVIOT, ABERDEENSHIRE

Start Loanhead of Daviot
car park, 5 miles
north-west of Inverurie
near Daviot village
Site location NJ747288,
OS 1:25,000 Explorer
map 421, Ellon &
Inverurie
Distance 200 yards
Time 30 minutes
Difficulty Easy
Family friendly

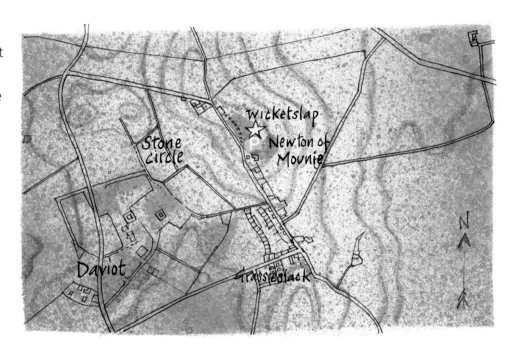

The Loanhead of Daviot is one of the most impressive recumbent stone circles, a distinctive type of Neolithic stone circle unique to Aberdeenshire in the north-east of Scotland. Almost a hundred of these circles survive, all of which have a massive recumbent stone flanked by two tall stones.

The majority of those with public access are not on prime walking land so are best visited as individual stops, but the lack of walking should not put off anyone wishing to discover some of Britain's most intriguingly designed stone circles.

The modern approach to Loanhead of Daviot is unlikely to bear any relationship to the original routes taken by the prehistoric builders and worshippers. You wander up to the circle from the west through woodland which surrounds the circle on three sides and is thickest to the south-west, somewhat ironically as we will see. You come out into a rectangular clearing beside the circle's recumbent stone. The wider countryside around is a fairly level landscape of intensively farmed fields, though views are restricted solely towards the north-east.

The massive 12-tonne recumbent stone was the first stone of the circle to be dragged and levered here approximately 5,000 years ago. The circle builders carefully laid it down on the south-west side of an area they had already prepared by making it level. They took great care and effort to make sure that the top surface of this huge stone was exactly horizontal then framed it by erecting standing stones at its two ends. They then added eight smaller standing stones to create a circle almost 20 metres (66 ft) in diameter. Cremated burials and fragments of pottery were placed in the pits dug to hold these stones upright. They either marked one stone with cup marks or reused it from an earlier monument such as a chambered tomb.

The builders were a small community living and farming the land in the surrounding area, and the annual solstices were apparently not important

enough astronomical events for the Neolithic communities of this part of Scotland. They had created an arena for ceremonies to mark a very particular lunar event known as the major standstill which only happens every 18.6 years. The angle between the moon's orbit and the earth's equator gradually increases over 9.3 years then decreases again over the same time period. During the year of the major standstill, the angle is at its greatest and

the full moon nearest the winter solstice appears at its highest point in the sky, while the summer full moon its lowest point. This summer full moon barely rises above the horizon in northern latitudes and appears to skim along the horizon.

Like nearly all recumbent stone circles, Loanhead is thought to have been built to create a false horizon from which to observe this summer full moon when it appears to run along the ground. If the Neolithic

Loanhead of Daviot is a distinctive type of Neolithic stone circle found only in Aberdeenshire

community did watch the summer full moon from the other side of the circle, the plantation now sadly totally blocks this sight.

Some time after the circle was built, its interior was filled with a low cairn of small stones within a low stone kerb. Another 1,000 years or more later, during the Bronze Age, another cremation area was built beside the circle. Cremated burials in urns were buried beneath low stone cairns and the cremated body of a man was buried in a hollow under his

funeral pyre in the centre of the area marked by two low curving lines of stones. The circle was probably no longer used to observe the moon sets by this time, but was still an important enough landmark for the community living in the area around it to bury their important dead alongside it without wanting to disturb its hallowed ground.

RIGHT *One of the tall stones at the southern end of Loanhead's recumbent stone*

NORTHERN ENGLAND

FROM GOATS TO KINGS
YEAVERING BELL, NORTHUMBERLAND

Start Gefrin monument
lay-by on the B6351
west of Wooler

Site location NT928293,
OS 1:25,000 Explorer
map OL16, The Cheviot
Hills

Length 2½ miles

Time 2 hours

Difficulty Difficult

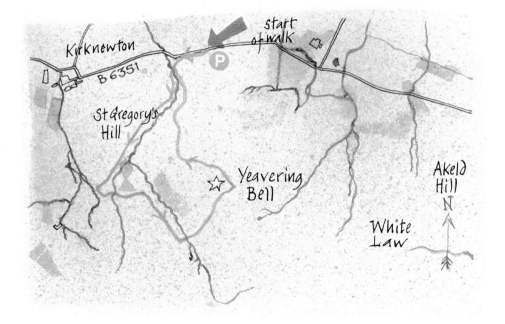

*The twin peaks of Yeavering Bell from
below the main gate into the hillfort*

Yeavering Bell is an Iron Age hillfort with a stone rampart encircling the distinctive twin peaks of a prominent hill in the east of the Cheviots. A clearly waymarked track takes you through the hillfort's main entrance, where you can explore the ramparts and house platforms, as well as look down on one of the royal palaces of the Northumbrian Anglo-Saxon kings.

Little is known about Yeavering Bell, a hillfort excavated over 100 years ago, though the remains of its sturdy ramparts and traces of round houses can be readily seen. The hillfort is thought to date from 500 BC, although how long it was inhabited is unknown.

The hill's double-peaked summit is visible from the start of the walk, which continues past the hill before crossing the stream and making the slow, gradual climb. As you climb, the bulk of Yeavering Bell keeps rearing above you, the closest peak rising seemingly vertically above the unrelenting slope. It is soon clear that a community living on this hill would feel pretty secure from attack and fairly self-important.

We finally break the slope below the original entrance through the ramparts and, with some relief, are on less steep ground. The rampart is a tumbled wall of quarried stone over 2 metres (6½ ft) wide around the top of the slope. It would have formed a tall pink wall completely encircling the hill, the local andesite stone only weathering to more of a grey colour after a few years' exposure to the elements.

Today you encounter a bleak open summit of sheep-grazed coarse grassland. Over 2,000 years ago when the hillfort was at its zenith, there would have been a village of 130 or so timber round houses covering most of the interior. Although much of the land had been cleared of woodland earlier in prehistory, in part leading to the formation of the moorland, there were still plenty of mature trees in the surrounding valleys to supply the timber used to build these houses. It is likely that this woodland was carefully managed by the local Iron Age communities. Traces of the platforms terraced into the sloping

The andesite of Yeavering Bell's ramparts still holds some of its pink colour, which would have formed a bright circle around the hill when newly built

summit to support the houses can still be found if you search them out.

Walking around the ramparts is the best way to appreciate the hill and the spectacular views, which take in the Cheviots to west and north, and the North Sea to the east. Many of the nearby hills are heather-clad peat moorland, which was already beginning to form when the hillfort was built. The Iron Age residents of Yeavering Bell would have looked down on a patchwork of fields and woodlands, the closest their own familiar farmland. Smoke rose from the houses clustered on many of the surrounding peaks, for this is a land where hillforts were never far apart.

Were the Iron Age communities driven to live on the summits because of a fear of attack, or because they wanted to communicate their importance to each other? The hillfort seems to have been abandoned during the Roman period, though there is little evidence for when the people left the summit to live elsewhere.

The fields around the Gefrin Monument below the hillfort to the east provide a link between prehistory and the early history of the Anglo-Saxons. Archaeologists had been looking for the Northumbrian royal palace of Adgefrin, mentioned in Bede's *Ecclesiastical History of the English People* as the place where Bishop Paulinus of York visited King Edwin and Queen Aethelburg in

Goodbye to Yeavering Bell

AD 627. Gefrin is a British place name, meaning Hill of the Goats, which was subsequently anglicised to Yeavering and, as the name surely refers to Yeavering Bell, the nearest hill, it suggests the hillfort had long been abandoned by the seventh century AD.

Cropmarks were spotted in the fields north of Yeavering Bell during the 1940s then excavated by archaeologist Brian Hope-Taylor in the 1950s. Hope-Taylor discovered a timber-walled enclosure, a sequence of large timber halls, the post holes of a tiered wedge-shaped auditorium and numerous smaller rectangular buildings and burials. This was the Anglo-Saxon royal palace, probably built at the site of a traditional British ceremonial centre so that the Northumbrian kings could meet regularly with local British communities and assert their authority.

These communities may have been the descendants of the hillfort's inhabitants who, over the following generations, would become slowly assimilated into Anglo-Saxon society. The need of the Northumbrian kings to demonstrate their authority in this part of the Cheviots had clearly subsided when Bede came to write his history as Adgefrin was abandoned by that time.

The descent which takes you down towards Gefrin and through 1,000 years of time begins on rocky steeps around the upper reaches of the hill before ending in the gentler valley below.

ENCIRCLED BY MOUNTAINS
CASTLERIGG, CUMBRIA

Start Keswick
information centre

Site location
NY291236, OS
1:25,000 Explorer
map OL4, English
Lakes – North West

Length 3.7 miles

Time 2 hours

Difficulty Moderate
Accessible

Castlerigg stone circle is set in one of the most visually stunning locations of any of the prehistoric monuments in Britain. A visit to Castlerigg gives panoramic views of some of the finest northern Lake District fells, including Blencathra, Helvellyn and Skiddaw.

This walk takes you out from nearby Keswick on to the pastures of the Castlerigg plateau, so that you can enjoy these views and appreciate why this location was chosen for the stone circle over 5,000 years ago.

The route from Keswick along Ambleside and Springs Roads to Castlerigg Farm is a gentle uphill stroll, running in part alongside a wooded beck. You are then on the southern edge of the plateau and approaching the – as yet unseen – stone circle. The lie of the land, as well as a dry-stone field wall, hides the circle from view until you are almost upon it.

The circle builders made this planning decision in order to heighten anticipation among people gathering here to participate in ceremonies. They also chose relatively small stones and were not making the same sort of grand statements as the people who built Stonehenge, Avebury, Callanish or the Ring of Brodgar.

Castlerigg's size, at 30 metres (98 ft) diameter and the height of its stones (as well as the density of circles locally) suggest that this was a place for more local gatherings of families from the surrounding area, as were the majority of prehistoric stone circles in Britain and Ireland. Ceremonies, and the circle's construction, were likely to involve more than just one family, but probably did not draw in large numbers of people from over a vast distance. Perhaps the communities who worshipped here came from the landscape defined by the ring of fells forming the horizon.

It was created some time around 3000 BC, towards the end of the Neolithic period, when the valleys below the plateau were probably mostly wooded, broken in places by clearings where farmers grew cereals and raised livestock. The higher fells were largely cleared, though thickets of rowan, hawthorn,

Looking across Castlerigg to the central Lake District fells and the route south. The stone circle's entrance is framed by the two largest stones to the left

birch and other native deciduous species probably covered the lower fells. These days, the valleys are largely pasture fields with some woodlands, giving way to open fells dominated by rough grassland and bracken.

Today, the wall around Castlerigg forces visitors to approach from the narrow road to the north. This may be along one of the original prehistoric approaches, as it brings you directly to an opening in the circle framed by the two largest stones, each about 2.3 metres (7½ ft) high. Each of these is flanked by lines of shorter stones forming something like a mini façade. Inside the eastern edge of the circle is a small square area defined by rows of standing stones; this was presumably a focus for ceremonies.

As you approach Castlerigg, you notice how, by carefully positioning the circle on the plateau top, which drops away immediately beyond the circle's far edge, the low ring of stones is elevated above a natural amphitheatre. The eye is drawn across the circle to the surrounding fells with their craggy skylines, which fold down one on top of the other into the gorge leading south to Thirlmere and the heart of the mountains.

This view leads towards the 24 km (15 mile) route to the Langdale Pikes, where Neolithic people quarried and flaked axes out of the fine-grained volcanic greenstone forming the steep cliffs and screes high up on Harrison Stickle and Pike o' Stickle. The quarry was difficult to access, simply a narrow ledge wedged between the rocky summits and the precipitous valley side at about 500 metres (1,640 ft) above sea level, so

the effort to acquire the stone to make these axes was significant.

These were not just any old ordinary tools for locals to fell trees with; rather they were prized possessions that were exchanged, both as roughly worked blanks and as finished polished axes, throughout Britain and Ireland. Some axes are worn through work, and were probably used bound into a wooden stave to clear woodland or till the soil, while others are found in pristine condition, often carefully deposited in ditches or burials, suggesting that the axes had a cachet about them as esteemed objects beyond practical use.

The people who quarried the axes, endangering their lives in the quest for the best stone high in the mountains, would have shared some of that elevated status, and they may have come from throughout the Lake District fells to take their share of the gifts of the earth in the high-risk semi-ritualised act of turning rocks into axes at what was surely a sacred place. Were any of these people from the same communities which built Castlerigg? Its proximity makes it tempting to think that they may have been, although if so they probably shared Langdale with the communities that created the other large stone circles in Cumbria, such as Swinside and Long Meg and Her Daughters.

The people who worshipped at Castlerigg would have been networked into these other communities. This is made clear on the return to Keswick, which brings you alongside the River Greta, a rushing beck forming below the two gracefully rounded fells of Lonscale and Blease on the approaches to Skiddaw and Blencathra. Greta runs along a valley that provides a natural lowland route east out of the fells and into the Eden Valley, where Long Meg and Her Daughters are only a day's walk away.

BELOW *The north-facing entrance of the stone circle.*

OPPOSITE *The stones of Castlerigg are local Skiddaw slate*

WITCHES' COVEN
LONG MEG AND HER DAUGHTERS, CUMBRIA

Winter sunrise over Long Meg

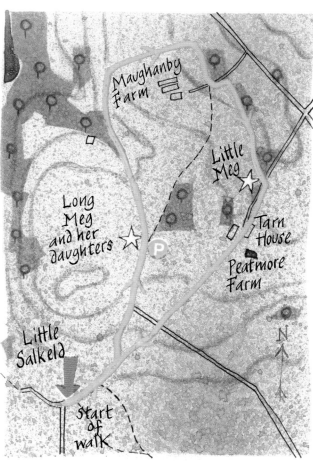

A weight of awe, not easy to be borne,
Fell suddenly upon my spirit – cast
From the dread bosom of the unknown past
When first I saw that family forlorn.

> William Wordsworth on Long
> Meg and Her Daughters

Long Meg and Her Daughters are often overlooked by visitors, who tend to gravitate to Castlerigg over 27 km (17 miles) to the west. This is a shame because the largest stone circle in northern England has a more evocative atmosphere, especially when the light begins to fade and nearby trees turn into silhouettes.

The circle was built about 5,000 years ago during the Neolithic period, roughly contemporary with Castlerigg, and Long Meg is one of only a handful of

Start Little Salkeld
Site location NY571372, OS 1:25,000
   Explorer map OL5, English Lakes – North
   East
Length 2.8 miles
Time 1½ hours
Difficulty Moderate
Accessible

standing stones with prehistoric rock art carved into its surface. A walk to see her is made all the more special because she stands off the beaten track above a wooded valley.

Little Salkeld is a pretty little hamlet, one of many spread along the Eden Valley, where Cumbria's only working watermill making stone-ground flour can be found near to a Victorian viaduct that once carried trains from Penrith to Carlisle. The walk to Long Meg takes you up a gentle hill on to a plateau on top of an escarpment above the River Eden. The minor road and lanes take straight routes with right-angled bends through a regular pattern of ruler-like walls and hedges, built and planted here about 200 years ago to enclose common grazing land on a low-lying moor, and create improved fields for the new model farms scattered to the north of Little Salkeld.

You arrive at Long Meg and Her Daughters suddenly. The stones seem to spring out of the ground just beyond a field wall, and it is difficult to perceive the scale of the circle. Long Meg is unmistakable - an angular red sandstone monolith standing aloof

LEFT *The side of Long Meg seen from inside the stone circle is decorated in prehistoric cup marks and concentric circles*

BELOW *Long Meg from inside the entrance of the stone circle with snow-covered Lake District fells in the distance*

from the ring of rounded grey glacial erratics, yet she leans in to listen in to the conversation.

Long Meg's rock was laid down as desert dunes between 250 and 300 million years ago and forms a great swathe of bedrock around Penrith. The same stone also appears in many of the town's buildings. At least four sets of cup marks and concentric circles have been pecked into the north-east facing side of the 3.6 metre (12 ft) high monolith, although whether they were created once it was erected here or before is unknown.

You will find the rock art on the side of Long Meg, which you pass to walk into the circle through an entrance defined by four stones set in a square. The circle extends beyond you, dropping slightly downhill to the right of the entrance, to complete a circuit of fifty-one stones almost 100 metres (330 ft) in diameter. Trees, the farm road, fallen stones and the slope combine to lessen the impact of the circle, despite its being over three times the size of Castlerigg, so you really need to walk the circumference to appreciate it fully.

The entrance faces south-west and long ago, the select few people standing inside the circle would have watched the sun set over or beside Long Meg, looking towards the side decorated with rock art, on the night before the midwinter solstice. The longest night was upon them and, if the gods were kind, the sun would be reborn the next day to begin the long slow journey further and further north, higher and higher into the sky towards spring and new life. There are views down the Eden Valley as well as to the Cumbrian fells to the west, though it cannot match the dramatic amphitheatre of hills around Castlerigg.

The walk continues north beyond Long Meg and Her Daughters across a massive ditched enclosure abutting the circle, which is buried underground and identifiable only as a cropmark. You follow bridleways and footpaths through the enclosed farmland to pass by another, smaller stone circle, known appropriately as Little Meg. One of her stones is also decorated with concentric circles and a spiral.

Legends have wrapped themselves around Long Meg and Her Daughters like the morning mist. Long Meg is named after a local witch, Meg of Meldon, who lived here during the early 1600s. Meg and her daughters were thought to be a coven of witches turned to stone by a medieval Scottish wizard called

Michael Scot – and if you can count the number of stones correctly you will break the spell or hear Meg's whisper.

It is not surprising that stone circles were often associated with petrified witches, as it was a way for the Church to demonise these ancient sites in an attempt to prevent them becoming centres for pagan revivalism. One outcome of this use of folklore to marginalise stone circles is the number of circles ascribed female names. Long Meg and Her Daughters is perhaps the most evocative of these, but you can find Nine Ladies, Seven Sisters and other groups of stone 'witches' across Britain and Ireland.

Some of Long Meg's daughters, looking south-west from inside the circle

MOTHER MOUNTAIN
MAM TOR, DERBYSHIRE

Start Castleton
Site location
SK150829, OS
1:25,000 Explorer
map OL1, Peak
District – Dark Peak
Distance 7½ miles
Time 4 hours
Difficulty Difficult

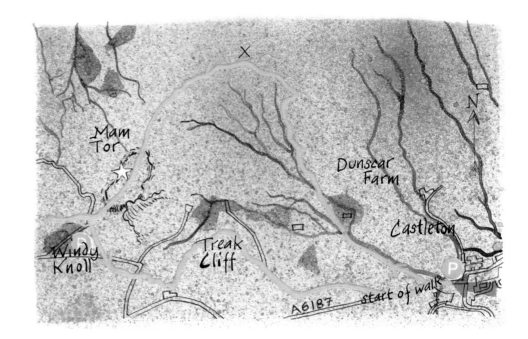

Mam Tor perches 517 metres (1,696 ft) up on a ridge marking the boundary between the White and Dark Peaks of Derbyshire. The ramparts of the late Bronze Age/early Iron Age hillfort are draped around the windswept hill, its summit dimpled by the platforms of round houses.

The hill is often so cold and windy that many visitors wonder why on earth people chose to live up here, rather than down in the more sheltered Hope Valley beneath. But when Mam Tor was built and occupied about 3,000 years ago, the valley was very different from today.

To really appreciate why the Mam Tor hillfort was built where it was, we will begin our walk in the valley at the picturesque village of Castleton. From Castleton you can see the looming bulk of Mam Tor rising at the head of the Hope Valley, the highest of a chain of hills that encircles the valley. The hills to the south form the northern limit of the White Peak's rolling limestone plateau and are clothed in grey-green grass, while the hills to the north are strung along a shale/gritstone ridge, which has a darker hue of rough moorland grasses and bracken.

Castleton is a small village of eighteenth-century cottages and grand Victorian villas. It was founded by the Anglo-Saxons, probably some time between the sixth and ninth centuries AD, then remodelled by the Normans in the eleventh century. William Peverel, an illegitimate son of William the Conqueror, built his castle on the rocky promontory above and the castle's twelfth-century grey limestone keep still towers ominously over the village.

Head out of the village towards Hollins Cross on the gritstone ridge to the right of Mam Tor, taking the footpath via Dunscar Farm. You pass through the traces of early medieval strip fields preserved by the lines of dry-stone walls built later in the medieval period to consolidate the strips into fields.

The bottom of the valley is mostly heavy and damp clay soils, so they would have been largely uncultivated until good drainage and steel ploughs were introduced after the Romans arrived in AD 43. This means that 3,000 years ago you would be wading your way through thick scrubland of damp-loving alders and willows rather than strolling through today's open landscape.

Mam Tor hillfort rises to crown the ridge between Edale and th e Hope Valley

Whereas today you can look up over open countryside to see the outlines of Mam Tor's ramparts, 3,000 years ago you would have caught only glimpses of its stone and timber walls through gaps in the trees. The distinctive landslip that scars its eastern flank, and gives Mam Tor its alternative name of the

Shivering Mountain, may not have collapsed when the hillfort was occupied. Climbing towards Mam Tor would have led us through thinner woodland until we eventually broke through onto open ground near the top of the ridge.

As you climb the side of the ridge up to Hollins

Frosty dawn over the Hope Valley seen from Mam Tor

Cross, the ground to either side drops straight down to the valley bottom. You feel like you're on top of the world, with views down to the Hope Valley and Edale far below to either side, both filled with green pastures divided by walls and hedges, small villages and individual farms. The dark-brown hulk of peat and heather-clad Kinder Scout challenges the walker on the skyline to the north of Edale, and radiates purple in late summer when the heather is in flower.

The ridge itself gradually climbs ahead until it reaches its summit at Mam Tor, where the ground is raised up to form a wider plateau. The grassed-over ramparts would have been even more prominent as high stone walls when newly completed. The public footpath runs along the line of an ancient track which certainly existed in prehistory. Perhaps the hillfort was built on this prominent location across a long-distance route by a group of people who wanted to show their strength and to control access along the route.

As you get nearer to the summit you notice a narrow nick carved in the skyline, which marks the location of the hillfort's north-east entrance. Today you can saunter through the entrance along a paved footpath, but in prehistory the way would have been barred with formidable wooden doors. The imposing boundary that enclosed the 16 acre (6 hectare) hillfort began life as a timber palisade and was later replaced by stone walls.

From the summit, you get stunning views east along the whole length of the Hope Valley, with the ridge of gritstone peaks you have walked along snaking away to your left, Castleton way below, Peveril Castle standing proud above the village and the Winnats limestone gorge in front. Immediately below you the landslip has dumped its shale and rock into a range of undulating hillocks which tumble beneath the hill and are crossed by the broken tarmac of the now-abandoned road.

If you look closely at the summit's grassy slopes

inside the ramparts you can spot some of 100 or more oval platforms terraced into the ground. Each platform was the floor of a small, timber round house about 5 metres (16 ft) in diameter that had a clay-covered timber and hurdle wall supporting a thatched conical roof of heather, bracken or straw.

Excavations in the 1960s led to the discovery of fragments of broken pottery vessels scattered around central hearths inside the houses. The large numbers of round houses suggest a large population living in an extensive hilltop village, though it is possible that not all of the platforms were occupied by houses at the same time.

The summit of Mam Tor is crowned with a burial mound approximately 1,000 years older than the hillfort, which is now covered by modern stone sets and spiked through its centre by an Ordnance Survey trig point.

Continue past the trig point to begin your descent, which takes you across the ramparts above the

south-west entrance and down on steps to the road from Castleton to Edale via Mam Nick. You should take a short diversion on to Rushup Edge to follow the approximate line of the prehistoric route as it continues west. Mam Tor appears to stand out alone as a separate hill from here, and you can see how the hillfort's summit rises magnificently from north-east to south-west.

From Rushup Edge you can drop down into the Hope Valley via a footpath which takes you close to the bottom of the landslip and via a steep descent over a dramatic limestone scarp punctuated by caves and mines dug for lead and the famous local semi-precious mineral, Blue John.

Below the scarp and past the landslip you are once more in the gentle ground of the valley, passing through dry-stone walls on your way back into Castleton.

Mam Tor hillfort, on the highest hill of a ridge which may have been a prehistoric long-distance route

FALLEN IDOLS
ARBOR LOW, DERBYSHIRE

Start Moor Lane
car park west of
Youlgrave
Site location
SK160636, OS
1:25,000 Explorer
map OL24, Peak
District – White Peak
Length 5½ miles
Time 3 hours
Difficulty Moderate
Family friendly

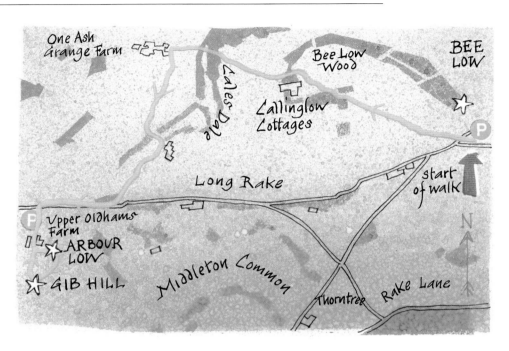

Some Neolithic henges are more enigmatic than others, and the fallen limestone circle of Arbor Low in the Peak District raises plenty of questions. We think it was built around 2500 BC, but the clockface-like arrangement of grey stones marking the inner edge of an artificial plateau within a bank and ditch attract much speculation – were they pushed over by the medieval Church or by superstitious farmers? What ceremonies were carried out hidden from view in the central cove? Did the stones ever stand upright in the first place? Then there is the question of who is buried in the early Bronze Age mound planted right on top of the bank in a landscape studded with ancient burial markers.

Before we search for answers to these questions at Arbor Low, it is a good idea to approach the henge in the way that Neolithic worshippers approached it – by walking across the White Peak. One significant point about the henge's location is that it is positioned on a north-facing slope just below the summit of a low plateau on Middleton Common. Arbor Low is tilted towards the lower ground of the Monyash Basin at the head of Lathkill Dale, towards which

one of the henge's two entrances face, suggesting that ceremonies held here were for and by people who lived in and around this large natural bowl. It is important to walk towards Arbor Low from this direction to begin to understand its importance to Neolithic communities of the White Peak.

The path from Moor Lane car park soon passes the burial mound of Bee Low on the right, though it is masked under the tip of a long plantation snaking up from Lakthill Dale. The mound is about 4,000 years old, dating from the early Bronze Age, and contained a number of burials with beakers and a flint arrowhead. Look around at the hilltops and you will see many with tiny pimples on them, nearly all of which are all early Bronze Age burial mounds. Certain important individuals were chosen by their communities to represent them after death. The prominent burial places were permanent reminders of the groups' rights to live and farm the land, and helped to create community histories by linking the living to their ancestral pasts.

We are walking through a highly organised farm landscape of ruler-straight limestone dry-stone walls and improved pastures for dairy herds and sheep. This land was open heathland until relatively recently, maybe 150 or 200 years ago, and villagers from Youlgrave held common rights to graze their livestock here. Then the landowners decided that the land needed to be improved, made more productive so that higher rents could be collected and the national good served through better land management. They extinguished common rights, enclosed the heath and had new farms planted among the new fields to grow new strains of crops and raise new breeds of livestock more efficiently.

That open heath had existed for thousands of years, at first intermingled with small woodlands until the trees were gradually cleared. To imagine the Neolithic landscape of Arbor Low, strip away the walls, lift out the regular plantations and replace the improved pastures with rough heathland and mixed deciduous woodlands of the sort found

BELOW *Arbor Low henge with the fallen limestone circle splayed out around the edge of the artificial plateau*

OVERLEAF *Looking through the north-western entrance of Arbor Low, across the fallen portal stones to the later burial mound built on the far side of the henge bank*

where the path crosses the steep dalesides of Lathkill Dale.

We now begin our steady climb on to the plateau, skirting the end of the dale to cross through more improved fields and pass by the occasional prehistoric burial mound. As we reach the road, begin to look out for the point where the large bank of Arbor Low forms a crest along the skyline and you will realise why Anglo-Saxons called it Eorthburg Hlaw, meaning 'earthwork mound'.

Fields without public footpaths on the other side of the road prevent us from walking directly up to the north-western entrance of the henge, so we must follow the road a little distance before entering Arbor Low via Upper Oldhams Farm. You can follow this road to return to the car park after visiting Arbor Low.

The modern approach brings us in to one side of the henge, an oval approximately 80 metres (260 ft) across surrounded by a 2 metre (6½ ft) high bank, which prevents anyone on the outside from seeing in. Scatters of Neolithic flints indicate that today's quiet field grazed by cattle and sheep would have been a bustling, noisy place over 4,000 years ago, as people gathered around the outside of the henge to meet beside camp fires, exchange tools, swap gossip and strike bargains over marriage partners while preparing for the ceremonies to begin.

To appreciate Arbor Low as these communities did during their ceremonies, bear left towards the field wall opposite the north-west-facing entrance. From here you can see the fifty-or-so recumbent limestone blocks through the wide entrance, framed on either side by the large banks circling around wide ditches between them and the stone circle. The ditch was hewn through the limestone bedrock some 4,500 years ago, using antler picks, some of which were carefully placed on steps in the ditches to either side of the entrances, before the spoil was piled up to build the banks.

Two stones lie flat in the middle of the entrance, as do another two in the entrance opposite, and it is these, along with the stones forming the central cove, that proved that the stones were designed to stand upright. They would have blocked the view into the centre of the henge, hiding ceremonies held there in much the same way as the outer ring of sarsens did at Stonehenge.

The tallest stones are two monoliths measuring over 2.5 metres (8 ft) at either side of the cove facing the entrances; clearly these were meant to shield the most significant ceremonies from those waiting outside the entrances. The circle was designed to create a sense of drama and mystery among the gathering as well as to delimit the ritual space. People may have been allowed inside the henge in a controlled manner, to witness or participate in certain parts of the ceremonies.

A striking feature when approaching uphill through the north-western entrance is the large burial mound silhouetted against the skyline on the far side of the bank. This was built here a few hundred years after the henge, at about the same time that other burial mounds were created on hill tops during the early Bronze Age. It contained a single individual buried inside a stone cist and appears to show that one family was making a claim of pre-eminence over the others by making the bold statement to take over one part of the henge to bury its own dead.

This is not the only burial mound at Arbor Low, and a short walk leads to Gib Hill, where there are two mounds built one on top of the other. The upper mound contained an early Bronze Age burial in a stone cist very similar to that in the mound on Arbor Low, while below was a much earlier long mound built over a burnt area of ground scattered with oxen bones. This dates from many centuries before Arbor Low and was probably created by some of the first farming communities, who constructed a number of these permanent mounds on seasonal upland pastures in the Peak District.

It shows that Middleton Common was already a ceremonial location prior to the henge and may be part of the reason that Arbor Low was built here in the first place, with the builders choosing a location with a long history as a place for grazing and rituals by semi-nomadic farmers. The family who built one burial mound on top of the other at Gib Hill clearly recognised the earlier mound as an important place, which suggests that it was a part of Arbor Low's sacred landscape when people gathered at the henge. We can't be sure whether they held ceremonies at Gib Hill too, or simply looked upon it as reminder of their ancestry, though it is likely that people did move between it and the henge during ceremonies at the latter.

OPPOSITE *Some of the fallen stones of Arbor Low*

THE FINAL POINT
RUDSTON MONOLITH, YORKSHIRE

Start Rudston
Site location TA098678,
OS 1:25,000 Explorer
map 301, Scarborough,
Bridlington &
Flamborough Head
Distance 1,000 yards
Time 30 minutes
Difficulty Easy
Accessible

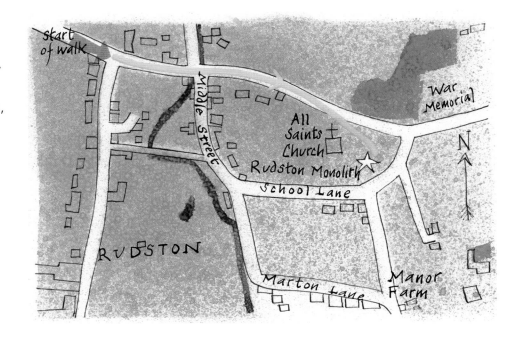

The tallest standing stone in Britain tells a story of medieval Christianity's fears of pagan revivalism. The Rudston Monolith is found inside All Saints' churchyard in the small East Yorkshire village of Rudston. Here, prehistoric and medieval worlds collide in a statement about the religious and cultural transformation of England.

All Saints' Church is obvious as soon as you arrive in the village. Its secure, squat form and square tower dominate the top of a hill above the houses. Like many Norman churches throughout the country, All Saints was built in a prominent location to proclaim the importance of Christianity. The short, gentle walk uphill allows glimpses of the church and its monolith through the trees.

The monolith has been in this place for 3,500 years or more, and was erected as a centre for Neolithic or Bronze Age ceremonies. It is an imposing 8 metre (26 ft) tall slab of gritstone, estimated to weigh between 26 and 40 tonnes. The antiquarians who probed the ground around the monolith in the 1700s estimated that another 8 metres were buried below ground. While this has not been proved beyond doubt, there must be a fair depth of stone underground to keep the monolith standing upright.

The standing stone was quarried from gritstone beds in Cayton Bay over 16 km (10 miles) away on the coast, then hauled up and on to the edge of the Yorkshire Wolds to be planted into the earth. It formed the focal point for a ceremonial and domestic landscape now lost below the later fields and houses. Two or three cursuses intersect at the monolith. These are long earthworks dating from the Neolithic period which may have been used for processions. A smaller standing stone and a cyst grave can also be found in the churchyard. The endeavour to quarry and successfully move this massive stone without cracking or fracturing it is a testament to the skills, organisation and vision of prehistoric communities.

It was the prehistoric movers of the monolith who first chose this prominent hill as a ceremonial centre. The Christian Church, realising not only the importance of the site but the Herculean task required to remove the monolith, chose to follow the lead of the prehistoric communities and build one of their own ceremonial centres right beside the stone. They aligned the east-facing gable of All Saint's nave alongside the monolith to demonstrate the dominance of the new religion over the old. Over time the memory faded of which came first, the stone or the church, and a legend gained ground that it was the Devil who threw the monolith at the church but missed.

Rudston, rather symbolically, brings us to the end of this prehistoric journey around Britain and Ireland. The emphatic full stop marked by the monolith and the incorporation of a major ancient ceremonial monument into a churchyard are metaphors for both the efforts prehistoric people went to create their cosmological worlds beyond subsistence and the need of the medieval Church to deal with these monuments from the past. In some places such standing stones were demolished and broken up, in others their ritual power was made subservient to that of the Church, while in yet others they were demonised through myths and legends as the work of the Devil.

While prehistoric monuments such as the ones we have walked around are rarely deliberately destroyed these days, their potential to attract thousands of people and generate countless stories still holds sway in the twenty-first century.

Rudston is the tallest prehistoric standing stone in Britain and one of a number incorporated into churchyards

FURTHER INFORMATION

There are many websites that provide plenty of information and photographs about the monuments contained in *Walk Into Prehistory*, along with thousands of other prehistoric monuments.

These two websites comprise directions, comments and photographs compiled by enthusiasts who, between them, appear to have visited almost every prehistoric monument in Britain and Ireland:

www.megalithic.co.uk

www.themodernantiquarian.com

Many of the monuments in this book are in the care of the national government heritage bodies who have websites giving visitor and historical information about their properties.

Cadw: www.cadw.wales.gov.uk

Dept of Environment, Northern Ireland: www.doeni.gov.uk

English Heritage: www.english-heritage.org.uk

Heritage Ireland: www.heritageireland.ie

Historic Scotland: www.historic-scotland.gov.uk

SELECT BIBLIOGRAPHY

Armitt, I. *Scotland's Hidden History* (The History Press, 2009)

Bradley, R. *The Prehistory of Britain and Ireland* (Cambridge University Press, 2007)

Cunliffe, B. *Iron Age Communities in Britain* (Routledge, 2009)

Darvill, T. *Prehistoric Britain* (Routledge, 2010)

McCaffrey, C. *In Search of Ancient Ireland: The Origins of the Irish from Neolithic Times to the Coming of the English* (New Amsterdam Books, 2003)

Ordnance Survey. Ancient Britain Historical Map, (Ordnance Survey, 2005)

Parker-Pearson, M. *Bronze Age Britain* (Batsford, 2005)

Pollard, J. (ed.) *Prehistoric Britain* (Wiley-Blackwell, 2008)

Pryor, F. *Britain BC: Life in Britain and Ireland Before the Romans* (Harper Collins, 2003)

Scarre, C. *The Megalithic Monuments of Britain and Ireland* (Thames & Hudson, 2007)

ACKNOWLEDGEMENTS

I would like to thank everyone who has helped to make this book.

All at Frances Lincoln for commissioning *Walk Into Prehistory*, including Andrew Dunn for guidance and keeping the production show on the road; Roly Smith, my editor, who unwound my ramblings and straightened my tangents, and Arianna Osti and Michael Brunström, FL's excellent designers, for making it all look so good. Georgia Litherland for commenting on parts of the text and my photographs, as well as for putting up with me disappearing for weeks or days at a time to visit all of the sites in this book.

Numerous people for helping with information and support – Peter Larson for access to Stonehenge. Mike Parker-Pearson for access to the Stonehenge Riverside Project. Mary Dunnet, Alan Jones and Paul Spence of Historic Scotland for access to Maes Howe and Skara Brae. James Naper for access to Carnbane West, Loughcrew. Phil Foley of Leitrim Tourism for guidance on footpaths around Carrowkeel. Bob Johnston for insights and maps for Ireland and Wales. Lionel Masters of the Department of Adult and Continuing Education, University of Glasgow and Jim McNeil of South Yorkshire Archaeology Service for information on the geology of Caithness. Andy Lines of South Yorkshire Archaeology Service for information on recumbent stone circles. Ciara Hayden of Sligo for modelling Cairn G at Carrowkeel. Jessica Dingfelder, Boillot Fabrice and family, Michael Hughes, and Kim and Tom McGuire for lively discussions at some of the monuments. Georgia and my daughter Kaya for playing at Chysauster.

INDEX

Frances Lincoln Ltd
4 Torriano Mews
Torriano Avenue
London NW5 2RZ
www.franceslincoln.com

Copyright © Frances Lincoln Ltd 2011
Text and photographs copyright © Bill Bevan 2011
Maps copyright © Martin Ursell 2011

ISBN: 978-0-7112-3177-1

Printed and bound in China

2 4 6 8 9 7 5 3 1